"I have loved Susie for a long time. I am always moved and strengthened by her walk with Christ and subsequent writings. In this new book, Susie gives us a fresh call to rise up and follow Christ with bold faith and humble hearts. This is a book for this moment in our history."

—Sheila Walsh, co-host of *Life Today*

"Susie Larson has done it again! With her winsome style, biblical roots, practical application, and from-the-heart communication, she's given all of us a clear pathway to fight the good fight, keep the faith, and run the race with endurance. I highly recommend it!"

—Chip Ingram, teaching pastor/CEO of Living on the Edge and author of *I Choose Peace*

"Captivating writing alongside challenging faith will ignite your desire to stand *Strong in Battle* in Susie Larson's latest. I underlined so many things in this interactive and practical book. Deeply encouraging."

—Tessa Afshar, *Publishers Weekly* bestselling author

"As children of God, we've always been in a battle, but many of us didn't realize its intensity until 2020. Now we know we've got to get our faith-boots fortified. This book is for such a time as now. Susie Larson is a fountain of 'spiritual intelligence.' As someone who learned to 'stand up' in my own soldier-boots through her wise counsel, I have walked with Susie as intercessor and friend for many years. I've witnessed her earning every drop of the rich encouragement you will glean from these pages. I don't know another soul who keeps marching through the trenches under heavy artillery with such confidence in God's promises—and with such integrity. (I've often also noted that her unique strength comes from having her husband, Kevin, standing beside her!) Everyone needs a friend like Susie to champion them on and help them walk victoriously through their own trenches. I highly recommend gathering sisters to grow *Strong in Battle* together."

—Kathy Schwanke

"Susie has been a longtime mentor to me through her writing and speaking but in recent years has become a dear friend. The way she lives her life in prayer, generosity, humility, and faith inspires me on an almost daily basis. She is a modern-day hero of the faith in my life. The Holy Spirit used this book to remind me how daily battles are won. Several times it reshaped my thinking and changed the course of my day for the better. No matter what you are facing, this book will help you win the daily battles in your life."

—Sarah Strand

"*Strong in Battle* is such a true source of wisdom, knowledge, guidance, and encouragement because Susie is speaking from a place of *experience*, and not theory only. The writings and testimonies come from the heart of a woman who has truly *encountered* the Living God in the center of her enduring battles, upheavals, injustices, and sufferings. Her writing is in such real time that sometimes I feel she is speaking out while in the middle of the boxing ring still actively engaged in throwing and receiving punches! In the midst of this, Susie has seen the Lord up close, heard the Lord's voice loudly and clearly, and most important, continues to lay her life down in surrender and sacrifice to gain the one thing that matters most—*true heart intimacy with the Lord*. Consistently living from that place, she is a clarion voice and a shining light. Her willingness to humble herself and bare her soul to her readers in a vulnerable way opens a floodgate of the very life, light, and love of Jesus, which becomes a touchpoint bringing forth healing! Her humility also allows her to issue bold and tough challenges to foster maturity in us as well. She is a rare treasure, and so is this book."

—Lynn Ferguson

STRONG
in battle

Books by Susie Larson

Your Beautiful Purpose

Blessings for the Evening

Blessings for the Morning

Your Sacred Yes

Your Powerful Prayers

Blessings for the Morning and Evening

Bountiful Blessings

Fully Alive

Blessings for the Soul

Prevail

Prepare Him Room

May His Face Shine upon You

Strong in Battle

Soul Care for the Battle

STRONG
in battle

Why the Humble Will Prevail

SUSIE LARSON

BETHANYHOUSE
a division of Baker Publishing Group
Minneapolis, Minnesota

Published by Bethany House Publishers
11400 Hampshire Avenue South
Minneapolis, Minnesota 55438
www.bethanyhouse.com

Bethany House Publishers is a division of
Baker Publishing Group, Grand Rapids, Michigan

Printed in the United States of America

Library of Congress Cataloging-in-Publication Data
Names: Larson, Susie, author.
Title: Strong in battle : why the humble will prevail / Susie Larson.
Description: Minneapolis, Minnesota : Bethany House Publishers, a division of Baker
    Publishing Group, [2022] | Includes bibliographical references.
Identifiers: LCCN 2022004813 | ISBN 9780764231711 (paperback) | ISBN 9780764240768
    (casebound) | ISBN 9781493437375 (ebook)
Subjects: LCSH: Christian life. | Spiritual warfare.
Classification: LCC BV4509.5 .L375 2022 | DDC 248.4—dc23/eng/20220301
LC record available at https://lccn.loc.gov/2022004813

Cover design by Emily Weigel

Author represented by The Steve Laube Agency

Baker Publishing Group publications use paper produced from sustainable forestry practices and post-consumer waste whenever possible.

22 23 24 25 26 27 28   7 6 5 4 3 2 1

For yet a little while and the wicked one will be gone
    [forever];
Though you look carefully where he used to be, he will
    not be [found].
But the humble will [at last] inherit the land
And will delight themselves in abundant prosperity and
    peace.
Psalm 37:10–11 AMP

Happy are those who hear the joyful call to worship,
    for they will walk in the light of your presence, LORD.
They rejoice all day long in your wonderful reputation.
    They exult in your righteousness.
You are their glorious strength.
    It pleases you to make us strong.
Psalm 89:15–17

CONTENTS

INTRODUCTION

I'm someone who has battled varying levels of fear my whole life. Praise God, I've come quite far in this regard. I'm not at all who I once was. I no longer live in that perpetual state of fight or flight, always bracing for impact. Though I still experience occasional bouts of fear, I now *live* with a holy expectancy because I'm learning to trust God more than I trust my circumstances.

Despite what the enemy seems to get away with in the world, God is always moving in our midst. Every time I look for God on the battlefield, I find Him there—in one way or another. God never claims neutrality. He's indifferent about *nothing*.

I've picked up on an enemy tactic, and understanding it might help you fight and win your own fear battles.

We're afraid to suffer, and the enemy knows this. We figure that if God has allowed us to go through the hardships we've already endured, what trauma must await us around the corner? Add to that stress the oversaturation of angry news and the vitriolic behavior on social media, and before we know it, our souls are ridden with anxiety. How do we begin to deal with the cultural decline when our own private battles already seem to be too much for us?

When we are not anchored to God's goodness, we are easy prey for the enemy. We often fail to realize that the enemy uses the pain of our past along with our fears of the future to build a case against God

The devil **wants** us to project our **fears** into a future that God is not in. But he **doesn't** get to do that.

in our minds. The devil wants us to project our fears into a future that God is not in. But he doesn't get to do that. The enemy is a liar. He's terrified that you'll finally get wise to his tactics. He wants you to forget that *absolutely nothing* can or will ever separate you from the profound and committed love of your Father (see Romans 8).

If you are in Christ Jesus, *He is in you*, which means there's no future part of your story where God is not present. When you embrace this truth, you can look back on your past hurts and remind yourself that they didn't get the best of you. And you can look at your present moment and know very well that God is with you here, giving you enough grace to take the next step, enough power, knowing that His Spirit resides in you, and enough purpose to impact the world around you.

You're still standing, and God is in the process of redeeming your story. We are in a battle. It's unwise to expect a life of ease in a day of war. Be wise to the enemy's tactics. Don't fall for his tricks. And don't confuse rest and replenishment with ease and apathy. God *will* still lead you beside peaceful streams. He's well able to restore your soul while the nations are in chaos.

God wants you to exude joy, belly laugh from your toes, and live with audacious generosity. He's also training your hands for battle. This is no time for numbed-out apathy, a life of perpetual leisure, or carnal pursuits that attach you to the things of this world. We need you in the kingdom! And your utter dependence on God *is* your superpower. The God who put the stars in place takes notice of every detail of your life. He is fierce in your defense. He tempers your storm, so you'll come through it more grounded in Him than you ever imagined. You can trust Him.

➤

When I first was called to write this book, I felt a bit like Jonah. Given my constant health challenges, I didn't want to pick a fight with the enemy and put myself in the line of fire. Not a heroic mindset, I know. Truth be told, I have to slay my inner sissy about five times a day. I bend toward self-protection when I'm not feeling well. But the more culture imploded all around me and fears rose up within me, and the more I heard cries for help in a way that felt beyond me, I knew the battle had amped up, which meant that we as God's people needed to rise up.

So I came up with a faith-declaration statement that I planned to build the book around (i.e., *As a citizen of the heavenly kingdom, I speak with precision, I pray with power, and I walk in authority*). I actually liked it a whole lot. But then I thought of Paul's words, *I put no confidence in the flesh*. Though my faith statements were biblically grounded, that approach didn't feel like the right strategy for me or for the times. My friend and I noted recently that when Joshua led the Israelites into the Promised Land, it was with a conquering mindset. And that was the Israelites' call for their time. But right now? Quite honestly, I see us more as a people who've been exiled to Babylon. We're called to thrive in Babylon like Daniel did, with a fear of God, deep humility, and profound wisdom.

In a day when people are in love with their own opinion and take constant liberties deciding who's in and who's out, we're putting our knees to the earth and our faces to the ground. Our battle is not against flesh and blood but against principalities and rulers in the heavenly realms. We have *one* enemy, and his name is Satan. On our own, on our best day, we're no match for him. He has studied us our whole lives. He knows our weak spots; he knows about our unhealed wounds and how to trigger our fears. We're like little children in the face of a Goliath of an enemy. Satan's not out to just poke fun at us; he wants to destroy everything that resembles Christ in and around us. But here's some *great* news:

> But you belong to God, my dear children. You have already won a victory over those people, because the Spirit who lives in you is greater than the spirit who lives in the world.
>
> 1 John 4:4

We won't spend a lot of time in this book overanalyzing the enemy's ways because I'd rather we spend that time strengthening our attachment to our perfect Father who promised to get us safely home. We'll explore the fear of God and the profound power of a humble heart. We'll be quicker to identify the enemy's predictable lies so we can overcome them with the truth. We'll sort through our fears, address our faulty mindsets, encourage our hearts, and then we'll stand in the authority that Christ has entrusted to us. We'll tear down every and any perspective that seeks to exalt itself above the knowledge of God.

I'm praying that by the time we're done here, you feel equipped, empowered, and encouraged to stand in faith, knowing you're going to see God move in His time and His way.

I've noticed that the more I rehearse the ways God has come through for me in the past, the stronger my confidence grows that He will carry me through, fight for me, and make a way for me in my current battle. I'm pretty sure we can say that all of our trials thus far have made us better, stronger, and more secure in Him, right? He tempers every storm and filters every attack so there's just enough opposition to make us stronger. The devil is on a short leash. And God has planted grace in every space!

One more thing: Pay attention when you read the Scriptures; notice where God's manifest presence is made known in ways people do not expect. Each time God shows Himself for who He actually is, all of man's self-striving and self-sufficiency go out the window. I want these stories to serve as reminders that God's majesty is beyond anything we can comprehend. Every knee will one day bow before Jesus because when the world sees Him as He actually is, *no one will be able to stand.*

We've gotten used to living without a strong sense of God's presence, and whether it's the result or a cause, we've lost our fear of God. But I believe with everything in me that that's about to change. May we humbly and reverently embrace the mystery of God. The King we serve does not fit in a tidy box or a predictable formula.

And He's not to be trifled with. Up to this point, I fear we've been too sure of ourselves and completely unsure of how mighty God actually is. Jesus is coming for a pure and spotless bride. If our battles don't purify us and make us more like Him, then what did they accomplish? My friend Thann Bennett writes,

> We have an irrational fear of the unknown . . .
>
> But for those of us who claim to believe in a God who supersedes and surpasses the bounds of our human minds, it is at the very least inconsistent to walk in fear of the unknown. It is a fear we need to unlearn. We need to unlearn it primarily because the unknown is where the mystery of God abides.[1]

The only way we're going to make it through these next few years is by growing more confident in God and less confident in ourselves. Bootstrap theology won't save us. But if we're willing to trust Him, we'll see our God move in ways that just might leave us breathless.

Let's raise a banner to the One who came and who is to come! Our King Jesus is coming for us. He commands us to stay engaged, keep our hearts in it, and live ready for His soon return. So let's live ready.

Living with Holy Expectancy,
Susie

HOW TO USE THIS BOOK

A quick note before we get started: At the end of each chapter, you'll find an opportunity for deeper study. I call it *Spiritual Intelligence Training*. This section is for those who want to do a deeper dive into Scripture. We'll learn from some of the conflicts and battles found in the Bible. *This section is purely optional and is ideal for Bible study groups and book clubs.*

Within each chapter, you'll find practical application tools to help you apply the truths you've just read to the battle you're currently facing; this is not fluff or filler, so please don't skip over this important content. *You'll need a journal* to work your way through these sections. (Consider the forthcoming companion guided journal, *Soul Care for the Battle*.) Here's a quick preview:

The Humble Way: We plan to approach our battles in the spirit opposite of what we're seeing in the world right now. We're going low. The degree to which we allow God to deliver us from our pride, striving, self-justification, and self-sufficiency will be the degree to which we walk in Christ's all-sufficient empowering grace. Pride gives the devil an open-door policy in our lives. Humility shuts the door in his face. God gives grace to the humble, He draws near to the humble, and He fiercely defends those who humbly fear Him. In this section, we'll explore the power of humility in every single battle we face.

Discern the Fiery Arrows: We put up with way too much from the enemy of our souls. In this section, we'll identify the lies, the harassment, and the attack he's aiming at you right now. When the battle is intense, it's easier to define, but it's often his subtle distractions that most often pull us off course. Here we'll learn to discern just what the enemy is up to so we can more effectively shut him down.

Say NO! Ephesians 6:16 reminds us that God has given us a shield of faith to block *every* fiery arrow the enemy sends our way. Your faith, coupled with God's Word, will change the trajectory of the battle every time. I like to say that our shield is how we tell our enemy, "Oh, no you don't!" This section will address ways to stand in faith and block the flaming arrows coming our way.

Say YES! Just as the shield is our way of saying, "Oh, no you don't!" our sword is our way of telling the enemy, "Oh, yes I will!" Your sword is your weapon of offense. Consider your current battle, and get a vision for what *overwhelming victory* might look like for you (see Romans 8:37). Here we'll get a sense of what God wants us to fight for and what He has for us up ahead. We'll learn how to stand on God's Word more firmly.

Therefore humble yourselves under the mighty hand of God [set aside self-righteous pride], so that He may exalt you [to a place of honor in His service] at the appropriate time.

1 Peter 5:6 AMP

ONE

The Battle Is Real

Stay Dependent

In the resurrection, Christ was victorious over the devil and his power. Therefore, Jesus Christ is the permanent ruler of the whole world; the devil is only the temporary ruler of the part of the world that chooses to follow him.[1]

Fear and panic jarred me awake in the middle of the night. Disoriented and in a cold sweat, I sat up in bed and looked around the room. Where was I? I shook my head to clear the fog, and then it came to me. I was out of state for a writer's conference and staying with a friend. Down in her basement. By myself. Terror gripped me. My neck prickled with fear. The room felt thick with an evil presence. A terrifying thought grabbed my heart and twisted it.

My youngest son, Jordan, was about to die. I could feel it. Didn't know how. Didn't know when. But the sensation was more real than my very breath. He wouldn't make it out of his twenties. I could barely breathe. I went to the floor, facedown, and cried to God for my son. *Oh, God in heaven, have mercy! Don't take my son at such a young age! Intervene. Guard and guide. Protect and provide!* I felt no peace. Only terror.

That is what I call a trauma fear. When the enemy comes in like a flood, hits you out of nowhere, and literally traumatizes you with a threat that takes your breath away.

Jordan was in his early twenties when I experienced this. He's now in his early thirties.

How do we discern the difference between a trauma fear and a God-given spiritual warning? One stirs up anxiety and a sense of dread, while the other inspires focused, passionate, faith-filled prayer. We'll talk more about that a little later in the book, but looking back, I realize that *I* was the one who gave the enemy access to torment me. Jordan had been in a wandering season, and it devastated me. The fears I'd left unchallenged within me gave the devil easy access to my soul.

We'd been so intentional (and so *not* legalistic) about following Jesus. We laughed together, enjoyed deep conversations about God, and kept it real at home. Our kids would tell you that they loved God and loved our home life when they lived under our roof. I was flabbergasted when Jordan decided to start partying instead.

The fear that gripped my gut eclipsed my faith. Knowing what I know now, I would have told that fear what's what and put my feet back on the Rock and prayed from my place of authority in Christ Jesus. Because I'd opened the door to fear, the enemy came in and took great advantage of the opportunity. Thankfully, in due time, I learned how to more effectively battle for my kids.

And just a follow-up note on Jordan: He is thriving. He's a wonderful husband, father, and son. Jordan regularly makes us laugh and honestly has more honor than anyone I've ever met. In some ways, he did experience a death of the flesh in his twenties. And he rose up to the life God has for him. The enemy threatened Jordan's life, but God redeemed it.

No matter where your fear and anxiety come from, Jesus cares deeply about your battle fatigue. He not only recognizes the reality of your battle, but He is also moved with compassion to help you move to a better place than you may find yourself in right now. Maybe your battle involves

- fear for your children's safety;
- prodigal children;
- acceptance (or rejection) of others;
- a troubled marriage;
- estranged family members;
- ill health in a tumultuous world;
- childhood trauma that still impacts you today;
- an accumulation of hard years;
- an acute trauma that actually happened (which has initiated your worst fears);
- your concern about society and where it will take us; or
- the battle within and your rogue thought life.

Or maybe yours is more of a global burden:

- the persecuted church
- widows and orphans
- poverty
- the unborn
- racial injustice
- human trafficking
- corruption in places of power
- unreached people groups

No matter where life finds you, no matter how the enemy opposes you, remember that Jesus loves you. *Deeply*. He cares about the burdens of your heart, and He's moved by the passion in your prayers. He's not only your Rescuer, but also your Redeemer; He's not only your Defender, but also your Deliverer. He intends to move you from victim to victor, from a defensive position of playing not to lose to an offensive position of running your race to win. He'll work mightily through every nuance of your story for His glory, for the enemy's defeat, and for your victory.

Jesus wants to transform you into someone you never dreamed you could be. He wants to turn your fear into faith, your tendency to self-protect into a passion to step out with purpose. He intends to train you to stand in battle not just for yourself, but for many who right now feel like they're on the losing side of their battle. You are part of a conquering army! When it's all said, the church will stand victorious. Your faith matters more than ever.

Wisdom in Warfare

To be clear, it doesn't always *feel* or *look* like Jesus is winning. But if we believe what we read in Scripture, we can show up to our battles with a strong assurance that God misses nothing, wastes nothing, and uses everything. He will one day turn the tables on our enemy and bring all things together under His glorious rule and reign. Our eyes will see it. Our hearts will rejoice. And we'll be glad we trusted Him.

Still, there's a cautionary word we must consider: Though God promises to get us safely home and use every bit of our story for His glory, that doesn't mean *we'll* automatically win every battle and come out of enemy skirmishes unscathed. Our enemy is cunning and would love nothing more than to batter us, berate us, and cause us to fall into one of his traps. Plenty of Christians take unnecessary beatings from the enemy and endure painful consequences as a result.

It's unwise and contrary to specific scriptural instruction to ignore the Holy Spirit's promptings and lean on our own understanding. When we don't fear God as we should, we trust ourselves way too much. How we fare in battle depends on how intimately we walk

How we fare in **battle** depends on how intimately we **walk** with Jesus.

with Jesus. He never made a move without the Father's input, and we must not either.

> A prudent person foresees danger and takes precautions.
>   The simpleton goes blindly on and suffers the
>   consequences.
>
> Proverbs 27:12

> Let your eyes look straight ahead; fix your gaze directly
>   before you.
> Give careful thought to the paths for your feet and be
>   steadfast in all your ways.
>
> Proverbs 4:25–26 NIV

So Jesus said to them, "Truly, truly, I say to you, the Son can do nothing of his own accord, but only what he sees the Father doing. For whatever the Father does, that the Son does likewise. For the Father loves the Son and shows him all that he himself is doing. And greater works than these will he show him, so that you may marvel.

John 5:19–20 ESV

The only way we're going to win our battles, the only way we'll ever thrive as an exiled people (until Jesus comes again), is if we walk intimately with God, stay profoundly connected to His Word, live yielded to His precious Holy Spirit, love others deeply from the heart (even when it costs us), and learn to rightly interpret our battles. We're on the winning side. Any defeat is temporary. Every pain will be redeemed. Every loss—in some way, shape, or form—will miraculously be restored.

In the meantime, we must accept the fact that, from here on, there's no room for disengagement or autopilot Christianity. Yes, God calls us to places of rest and replenishment, but always with our hearts engaged, our eyes upward, and our spirits yielded to the Spirit of the Living God.

We're on earth for a short time. And during this time, God invites us to trust Him more than we trust ourselves. We fix our eyes on what we cannot see because what we see is temporary. We lose our way (and our nerve) when we get so caught up in the temporary that we lose sight of the eternal. As the song says, "Jesus has never lost a battle, and He never will."[2] Whatever He allows in our lives, He intends to redeem. Our trials are achieving for us an eternal glory that far outweighs them all.

> That is why we never give up. Though our bodies are dying, our spirits are being renewed every day. For our present troubles are small and won't last very long. Yet they produce for us a glory that vastly outweighs them and will last forever! So we don't look at the troubles we can see now; rather, we fix our gaze on things that cannot be seen. For the things we see now will soon be gone, but the things we cannot see will last forever.
>
> 2 Corinthians 4:16–18

That's the goal, isn't it? To be utterly transformed by God's Spirit within us; for our spirits to be renewed day by day though outwardly all seems to be wasting away. The earth and everything in it will pass away. But we were made for eternity! Our setbacks are actually setups for that Great Day when God announces to all of creation that we belong to Him. The whole world will stand in awe when He reveals how He's been working marvelously behind the scenes (and sometimes quite publicly) to carry out His perfect plans for His people. Our God is meticulous and miraculous.

Eternity with Jesus will take our breath away: Unhindered intimacy with God. Abounding joy with no enemy opposition. Fellowship with our brothers and sisters as we share our awe-filled stories of how God intervened in our lives. Together, we'll marvel as we learn about all He provided and all He prevented, and we'll love Him even more than we did before. Jesus' desire to remember our faith-filled deeds and reward us for them will leave us utterly stunned.

If only we could live in such awe today because of those beautiful realities that await us. He makes note of our faith. He moves on our prayers. He rewards those who earnestly seek Him.

➤

Jesus promises in John 16:33 that on our journey homeward we'll see trouble. Even so, in the same verse, He tells us to "be of good cheer" (KJV), which means to grab hold of courage, take heart, and cheer up! How will the world ask about the hope within us if they see no hope within us?

Does living out that hope mean we slap on a smile while walking through incredible hardship? No. But it does mean that we dig deep, find the fortitude God has put in us, and resolutely fix our eyes on the One who is coming for us and who promises to redeem all things. Especially in this day of battle, we must throw off every shred of apathy and passivity and engage with intentionality:

- *Interrupt* every rogue, inferior thought, and make it bow and submit to Jesus (2 Corinthians 10:5).
- *Receive* God's kingdom power by faith (1 Corinthians 4:20).
- *Believe* that you will indeed be renewed day by day (2 Corinthians 4:16–17).
- *Yield* to the moment-by-moment influence of the Holy Spirit (Galatians 5:16).
- *Trust* that you can live with a joy that strengthens you (Romans 15:13).
- *Shine* brightly in a dark world that's lost its way (Philippians 2:15).
- *Be expectant* about eternity (Revelation 21:4).

Though the battle is real, God is greater still—greater than your fears, greater than your enemies, and even greater than the times we're in. God is developing a warrior in you! He's teaching you how to

We must **believe** we can be renewed day by day, live with a **joy** that strengthens us, **shine** brightly in a dark world that's lost its way, and live with a **holy expectancy** that heaven is real and goodness is **coming**.

persevere. And He wants you to know how to take care of your own heart. No doubt, some of your battles have taken a toll on your soul.

Don't go too long without acknowledging your need for repair, replenishment, and restoration. Are you offended with God because He allowed some prolonged trial? Hurt that He didn't intervene in a way you'd hoped He would? Are you holding a grudge against someone whose choices have made your life more difficult? Are you just plain exhausted from the fight? Have your fears made you timid and self-protective?

There's no shame here. No condemnation. Bring your whole self to Jesus—the mess, the fatigue, your hopes, and your dreams. Don't think for a moment that just because we're in a time of great spiritual battle, God doesn't care deeply about the desires of your heart. He does.

Ask Him to speak to you about His highest and best will for you. Ask Him to give you audacious faith and vision for your place in this holy race. *Invite Him to help you sort through your losses, hardships, and battle wounds in a way that brings newfound healing, strength, and even boldness.* Put a priority on your soul's restoration; it's the only way to last long and finish strong. Jesus loves to restore souls. And He's right here with you.

Prayerful Reflective Questions

1. *Father, I'm listening. How have my battles impacted me? What in me needs to be healed and restored?*
2. *Whom do I need to forgive?*
3. *How have my trials impacted my view of You?*
4. *What self-limiting and/or God-limiting beliefs hold me back from the best of what You have for me?*

The Humble Way: Our flesh surfaces when the battle rages. We all have stuff in us that needs to go. In Christ Jesus, our status before the King is secure. But our stuff is often what the world stumbles over. To be clear, the world also stumbles over the Jesus in us because many love the darkness more than light. But we never want to attribute persecution to our blind spots and selfish habits. We all have character flaws and fleshly tendencies that need to go. In ever-increasing measures, we must decrease, and Christ must increase.

Always remember, though, in this process, there's *never any condemnation* for you because you're in Christ and He's in you! The enemy is the one who wants to beat you down. Ever and always it's Christ who picks you up, holds you up, and draws you close. He invites you upward and onward, deeper into His heart for you and for the world. And in the process, He increases your capacity to know His love and power in a way that changes you. Don't be afraid of the searching work of the Holy Spirit. Yes, it's humbling. But never humiliating. There's stuff in you that you can't see, but Jesus sees and still loves you with a smile on His face. Such good news, no? However, the enemy is a legalist and he'll look for an open door within you to leverage every opportunity against you. Pray this verse with me, if you will, then write down anything the Lord brings up in you:

> Search me, O God, and know my heart;
> test me and know my anxious thoughts.

Point out anything in me that offends you,
and lead me along the path of everlasting life.
Psalm 139:23–24

Discern the Fiery Arrows: Our enemy is the author of confusion. He loves to confuse then accuse, to deceive and then defeat. Before we know it, we're so disoriented by the flurry of chaos that instead of standing in battle, we fearfully run for cover. We shift our gaze onto people and circumstances, and reason that if they wouldn't have or would have done this or that, we wouldn't be where we find ourselves now. Yet, in such reasoning, we discount the sovereignty of God. Yes, man's choices wreak havoc on the earth in ways big and small. But if we truly believe that our great God works all things together for the good for those who love Him and are called according to His purpose,[3] we won't spend our lives playing whack-a-mole reacting to things we cannot control.

Somehow, we need to find a way to release our fears and cares to God on a moment-to-moment basis so we can travel lightly and pray boldly. So back to the arrows. Once we're able to step back from the battlefield and remember that the Lord actually is in charge, we can better discern how and why the enemy is trying to take us out.

I've noticed for myself that at times, Satan shoots at unhealed areas that are easily triggerable. For example, it used to be that when specific neurological symptoms surged, my predictable emotional response was fear and then discouragement. Why? Because I never kept things in the present moment where God's grace was available to me. I'd connect current symptoms to old trauma and then project them into a fearful future. Each and every time, I'd crawl out of the ditch and repent for my lack of faith. Then my challenge was to accept His loving grace and not berate myself for stumbling in such a familiar way.

I used to despair over such weakness within me. Now I see it as a God-allowed battle that eventually gave me a strategy to shore up my life with more truth from God's Word—an invitation to heal on an even deeper level.

At other times, however, the enemy's arrows come at me with such fury that I know God is about to break through in some miraculous way. That is enemy opposition in its most predictable fashion.

I don't believe that Satan knows the future, but he's had time to study us, to watch God work, and to see God's angelic warriors mount up on our behalf. I think he senses when our breakthrough is just around the corner, and he pulls out all the stops to discourage us just beforehand. Our charge, then, is to take our stand, submit to God, and then resist the devil, knowing he has no choice but to flee.[4]

Pause now and spend some time with God. Ask Him to help you to discern the arrows aimed at you. Might they be

- rejection?
- fear of the future?
- abandonment?
- sickness?
- distraction?
- insecurity?

Discern the arrows and write them down; see them for what they are. You have one enemy, and he attacks in often predictable ways. But we're not going to put up with it any longer.

Say NO! As I mentioned in the book's introduction, the shield of faith is our way of saying NO to the enemy of our soul. God gave us this shield to block every fiery arrow the enemy sends our way.

> In addition to all of these, hold up the shield of faith to stop the fiery arrows of the devil.
>
> Ephesians 6:16

In this section, take some time to dig in to the Word of God and find your combat verses. Here are a few examples to get you started.[5]

Rejection or Abandonment:

> For the LORD your God is living among you.
> He is a mighty savior.
> He will take delight in you with gladness.
> With his love, he will calm all your fears.
> He will rejoice over you with joyful songs.
>
> Zephaniah 3:17

Fear:

I prayed to the LORD, and he answered me.
　　He freed me from all my fears.
Those who look to him for help will be radiant with joy;
　　no shadow of shame will darken their faces.
In my desperation I prayed, and the LORD listened;
　　he saved me from all my troubles.
For the angel of the LORD is a guard;
　　he surrounds and defends all who fear him.

Psalm 34:4–7

Sickness:

But he was pierced for our rebellion,
　　crushed for our sins.
He was beaten so we could be whole.
　　He was whipped so we could be healed.

Isaiah 53:5

Find a verse that speaks to your situation and that deeply resonates with your heart. Write it down. Memorize it. Say it, sing it, pray it.

Say YES! Consider your current battle and get a vision for what *overwhelming victory* might look like for you (see Romans 8:37).

Write down a corresponding verse that speaks to the promise of a great victory in your specific area of struggle. Then write it out in a paraphrased declaration. Here's an example:

> Yet I am confident I will see the LORD's goodness
> while I am here in the land of the living.
>
> Psalm 27:13

Paraphrased Declaration:

> My God is good, and His promises are true! Fear will not have the last say in my life. And I won't have to wait for heaven to get the victory. I *will* see His goodness in the land of the living. My heart is set on Him!

Personalized Prayer

Precious Lord,

I humbly bow before You, acknowledging You as my Savior and King. You know the battles I've endured and the wounds I've incurred. Heal me, Lord! Restore my soul and make me whole! Show me what lies I picked up when life let me down. Show me what's true. And reveal to me afresh my role in the greater kingdom story. Give me renewed faith to believe You for greater things in the days ahead. I don't want to shrink back in fear or fall down because I'm distracted. Awaken me to Your presence and power this hour. I'm so very honored to be an heir and a part of the coming kingdom. Help me to stay the course and to keep my heart in it. In Your precious name, I pray. Amen.

Spiritual Intelligence Training
WILL GOD MAKE A WAY?

1. When the spies initially scoped out the land *promised by God*, they came back with a fearful report (all but Caleb and Joshua). Their negative perspective infiltrated the camp. Read Numbers 13:25–33 and answer the following questions:
   a. The land God had promised was a good land. Even the unbelieving spies said so. What did the land offer them?
   b. What were the obstacles?

2. On the other side of every God-assigned battle is a promise. "Spiritual advance requires faith, and unbelief will never see beyond the difficulties. Unbelief sees 'walled cities and giants' rather than the presence and power of God. Unbelief looks at obstacles; faith looks at God."[6] Consider the power of a negative perspective. Conversely, ponder the power of a faith-filled one. How have naysayers kept you from stepping out and laying hold of something God had for you?

3. Read Numbers 14:1–4 and notice the crescendo of unbelief that takes place. When our fears become rebellious, we often do four things: 1. We glamorize the past. 2. We accuse God. 3. We project trauma and hardship into our future. 4. We construct a manufactured plan and take matters into our own hands. Based on this passage, write down the four ways the Israelites did these very things.

4. Time for some soul-searching. Consider the list above and prayerfully ask God to show you how fear and unbelief have compelled you to do the same things. (If you have them, give personal examples of these four points.)

5. Let's read Psalm 106:24–25:

> The people refused to enter the pleasant land,
>   for they wouldn't believe his promise to care for them.
> Instead, they grumbled in their tents
>   and refused to obey the LORD.

38

6. God made a promise to His people. He'd already performed miracles that had left them breathless. Yet when negativity, entitlement, and fear took root, the people sabotaged their destiny. We're saved by grace (see Ephesians 2:8–9), and God works all things together for the good of those who love Him and are called according to His purpose (Romans 8:28). Still, do you think a believer can miss the best of what God has for them? Write down your thoughts.

7. Someone once said, "There are only two things we should fear: (1) God, (2) nothing else." Read Numbers 14:5–44 and consider the contrast between men who humbly feared God and the masses whose fears had become rebellious. What stands out to you?

8. Dependence on God is everything. The abiding life is the miraculous life. Read John 15:5–8 and write it out as a personalized prayer.

TWO

Why Am I Facing Attack?

Stay in Rank

We mess around in prayer because we think it doesn't matter, when in reality we are sentries standing guard at the front lines of spiritual combat. It's easy to say, "Lord, bless me and my family. And by the way, thank You for this food. Amen." That's good, but it's hardly the kind of prayer that will cause Satan to tremble. It's time for all of us to raise the bar and enter into serious spiritual warfare.[1]

W hy is this happening to me?" whined the spoiled young woman as she traipsed through the rain, fussing over a broken nail. She had joined a mission trip to help the less fortunate but couldn't get over herself long enough to help anyone else. The villagers who lived joyfully within the simplicity of their circumstances were far richer than she, but she was too clueless to notice. To this day, I don't remember in what movie I saw this scene, but as you can imagine, it left a sour taste in my mouth. This stuff is easy to spot in others but is unfortunately not so easy to see in ourselves.

If pushed far enough, most of us will ask the same question: *"Why is this happening to me?"* We find ourselves in a raging storm with waves that threaten to topple us. We barely come up for air before we're pulled back under again. You think, *I could handle it if it were only one crisis,* but so often, it's when troubles come at us from every angle that we wonder where God is. One moment, we're doing life the best we know how, and the next, all hell seems to break loose on us.

Honestly, when I consider some of the things God has allowed in the lives of His children, I've struggled. I wonder why certain humble, God-fearing saints have to endure so much while others seem to live charmed, blessed lives serving Jesus where everything they touch prospers. It's one of the questions I'll look forward to processing with my heavenly Father someday. But right now, I hold fast to the truth that He is eternally good and that there's much I cannot see or don't have the capacity to understand. So I entrust my unanswered questions to Him, knowing that some great conversations await us and that the mysteries of this life will all make sense one day.

We all have different thresholds for battle, pain, suffering, and inconvenience. How far you have to be pushed before you pull the *Why me?* card seems directly connected to how much you've endured up to this point. Some people—like Job—can endure a whole lot before they ever think of blaming God for abandoning them. That kind of character and moral courage develops over time—one humble offering of trust at a time.

Even so, no matter the severity of your trial, it's human nature (and a legitimate question) to wonder, *If God could stop this, why doesn't He?* Not that we can demand answers from Him (He owes us nothing and has given us everything in His precious Son, Jesus), but God indeed welcomes our lament, our questions, and our doubts. His truth is sturdy enough to withstand our questions. Bo Stern writes,

We all suffer, but those who know Christ should suffer with hope so that a watching world can see that He is a very present help in times of trouble. We may wish for a God who will keep us out of all afflictions, but isn't it wonderful to become acquainted with the

One who goes with us into the heart of the fight, and then uses it for something beautiful?[2]

⤍

I've heard countless folks say that we need to stop asking *Why me?* and instead ask *Why not me?* That question is a great equalizer, wouldn't you say? Do you ever stop to wonder why God has been so very *good* to you? Why did He save you? Why is He willing to tend to some of the deepest desires of your heart? (Especially while national crises erupt all over the world.) He's not too busy to show up at your daughter's soccer game or meet you in your prayer time or shift the circumstances at work on your behalf. "Amazing love! How can it be"?[3]

But while considering your battles, I'd love to return to that first question and dare to ask *Why me?* Not with an entitled, whiny heart, but with a bold, brave, courageous spirit.

There's no one-size-fits-all strategy for battle, so it's wise to discern why and how we find ourselves facing opposition. Hugely important caveat here: This is not to say that we're always the ones who get ourselves into trouble. It's not to say that every battle is a result of our negligence or sin. And it's not a question that we should wield when someone else is in the trial of their lives. They don't need anything from us that sounds remotely like, "You know what your problem is?" Or "Maybe this happened because . . ." That's what Job's friends did. No. Discerning the reason for *our battle* is to determine *our battle strategy.*

Now when opposition comes, I go right to prayer. *Lord, why have You allowed this battle in my life? Have I given the enemy access in some way? Do I have a blind spot that he's leveraging against me? Or is the enemy blowing smoke because You're about to do something new, and he wants me to miss it? What do You want me to learn from this? What's my divine strategy for navigating this battle victoriously? Please show me what faith and obedience look like here.*

So, let's answer the question **Why am I facing attack?**

Because Jesus **loves** you, and the enemy **hates** you. Though God's promises and plans will ultimately **prevail**, the devil will stop at nothing to distract, discourage, or derail you from your **high calling** in Jesus Christ.

Let's take a brief look at a few storms and battles from Scripture and see if we can't glean some insight on the varying reasons we face the challenges we do:

- Naomi faced unimaginable loss because, in the face of a national famine, her husband led his family outside the boundaries God had set for them—*He looked for man-made solutions to a God-sized problem. He should have sought God for his people, but instead he wandered to find solutions for himself; people pay the price when we take matters into our own hands, and when we look to man for answers that we need to receive from God.*

- Jonah faced a storm (and the sailors with him) because he was trying to run away from God, not toward Him—*Jonah's storm was a consequence of his disobedience. People pay the price when we abdicate our God-given responsibilities.*

- Esther faced a life-or-death moment because God had groomed her and prepared her to stand in the gap for her people—*Esther's battle was the culmination of her divine calling. She did it right: She summoned people to fast and pray, then she prepared her heart and sought God and went forward in faith, and we're still talking about her today. Many Jewish people lived instead of died because one woman dared to stand in the gap as an intercessor and an advocate.*

- Jesus' disciples were in a storm because Jesus led them there to equip them for their ministry—*The disciples' storm served as a school of preparation. Jesus modeled rest (sleeping in the middle of a raging storm) and authority (speaking to the wind and the waves). There was a demon waiting for them on the other side of the lake, and ministry responsibilities were about to pick up; the disciples needed to know how*

45

*to both rest in God's authority and walk in God's power;
Jesus used the storm to teach His disciples and to teach us
how to keep our wits when the storms rage.*

- Paul and Silas ended up in prison because they confronted
  the evil in their day, yet God used the injustice to display
  His power and glory—*Paul and Silas were on mission; they
  bravely endured persecution and helped establish the early
  church. They turned the world upside down. Paul and Silas
  disrupted the status quo wherever they went; their battles
  were continuous and unrelenting, and we're still benefiting
  from their courage today.*

Get Back in Rank

Our enemy has been around a long time and has had countless
opportunities to study our weaknesses, take notes on our selfish
tendencies, and observe our unfulfilled desires. He knows how to
orchestrate situations that trigger our fears, ignite our jealousies,
and compel us to grab quick solutions. If we're out of step with the
Spirit, we're easy prey for the enemy.

> Submit yourselves, then, to God. Resist the devil, and he will flee
> from you.
>
> James 4:7 NIV

The word translated as *submit* here is a Greek military term that
means to come under the leader, to get back in rank. Watchman
Nee once said that we'll never have authority until we learn to come
under authority. Often, we open the door to enemy attack because
we've stepped out from under God's rule and reign in our lives. Too
often, we make light of nuanced attitudes and judgments against
others. We think nothing of picking apart our pastor's sermon or
gossiping about their kids, not realizing that we've set out the bait
for the enemy to launch his attack.

Often, we **open** the door to enemy attack because we've **stepped out** from under God's rule and reign in our lives.

Notice in the scriptural examples of storms and battles how profoundly people's decisions affect others. When we surrender our responsibility or embrace ungodly attitudes without any fear of God, we make ourselves (and others) vulnerable to enemy attacks. When we try to manufacture solutions on our own, we not only miss the wonder of God's provision, but others also pay a price for our disobedience.

That's why the Psalm 139 prayer is essential for every believer today. *Search me, O God, and know my heart! Test me and know my anxious thoughts. Point out anything and everything in me that offends You, and lead me in your everlasting way!*[4]

We need to give time and space for this prayer, time to listen and to respond to what the Lord speaks to our hearts. He may bring up an old grudge that you'd forgotten about but that has embedded in your soul and has kept you from moving forward into the things He has for you. He may nudge you to admit that you've made an idol out of your children, or that you're wasting too much time on social media, or that you've allowed jealousy to filter your thoughts and steal your joy. Whatever He shows you, respond, repent, and receive His unfathomable mercy and grace, which He so lovingly pours out at a moment's notice.

Once you're back under authority, now you have authority—Christ's authority. Here's where you rise up and *resist* the devil and his evil schemes against you, your family, and the culture at large. To resist is to oppose, to say no, to stand in faith in the authority entrusted to you and tell that enemy to stand down. The rest of the verse reads, "and he will flee from you."

Would you believe the word *flee* means that you'll have him running, seeking a place of *safety*? Think about it: The devil finds safe places in Christian spaces whenever we usurp authority and step out of rank. But when we humble ourselves under God's mighty hand, fear Him with reverence and honor, and serve Him on His terms in His way, well, then the enemy comes trembling from his stronghold, flees as fast as he can, and finds a place to dwell where he won't be disrupted. Wow. That's why Scripture says this:

The fear of the LORD is the beginning of wisdom,
And the knowledge of the Holy One is understanding.

Proverbs 9:10 NKJV

Prayerful Reflective Questions

1. *Father, have I stepped out of rank in any way? Show me my heart. Please show me what I need to see.*
2. *What are some of the most consistent ways I open the door to the enemy of my soul? (e.g., worry, fear, anger, sloth, etc.)*
3. *Whom do I need to forgive?*
4. *What's Your promise to me in this place? Please show me a word from the Word that I can lay hold of and make my own.*

The Humble Way: Sometimes we lament that we're weary in battle and yet we've ignored the exit ramps God has provided for rest and replenishment. His ways are not our ways. His thoughts are not our thoughts.[5] Especially in seasons of battle, we need to trust Him more than we trust ourselves. Let's look at this passage together and consider what the Lord might be saying to us today:

> This is what the LORD says:
> "Stop at the crossroads and look around.
>   Ask for the old, godly way, and walk in it.
> Travel its path, and you will find rest for your souls.
>   But you reply, 'No, that's not the road we want!'"

Jeremiah 6:16

There's an ancient path of wisdom before us, paved with the footsteps of the saints who've gone before us. They've learned well the lessons of rest, perseverance, and trust. Do you trust God more than you trust yourself? Are you willing to follow Him to a restful place when your schedule says it's impossible? Are you ready to let go of control, let people think what they will, and follow Jesus in a humble, trusting way? What about the façade of having it all together? Can you trade saving face for saving grace so that your soul can flourish again? Spend some time with God. May He show you how connected humility and rest are. To win in battle you must know how to rest in Jesus.

Discern the Fiery Arrows: We walked through the possibility of being out of rank. The truth is, even if our battle is an all-out enemy attack because we're doing so much for the kingdom, the possibility is always present that we'll lose our footing in reaction to the storms and trials we endure. So it's always an excellent exercise to work through.

Maybe you're under fire because you're making a difference in the kingdom. Your enemy hates it. He fights dirty and shows no mercy. But as I often say, you're not at the mercy of your trials (or your enemy); you're *in* the mercies of God.

Even so, the battles are real, so let's take some time to discern the lies and the threats the enemy is sending your way. Pause here for a moment. Put on some worship music and wait on the Lord. Prayerfully ask Him to help you name the arrows that have whizzed by you (or have hit their mark). Try to look past the circumstance and understand the enemy's motivation and intent. For instance, one day on my radio show, Holley Gerth shared that she asked God, *Lord, why does the enemy keep trying to steal my joy?* To which Jesus

You're **not** at the mercy of your **trials** (or your enemy); you're *in* the **mercies** of God.

replied in a gentle whisper to her heart, *He's not trying to steal your joy. He's trying to steal your strength*. Since the joy of the Lord is Holley's strength, the enemy thought he'd go after her joy. Once she figured out his scheme, she decided to go after the joy of the Lord, and the more she did, the stronger she became.

Discern the arrows and write them down; see them for what they are. You have one enemy, and he attacks in often predictable ways. But we're not going to put up with it any longer.

Say NO! In Luke 10:19, Jesus told us that He's given us authority over all the power of the enemy. He's given us authority; now we need to take authority and walk in it. But it begs the question: Do we have power to stop all suffering? I don't think so. Too many people still love the darkness more than the light, and in them the enemy finds easy access to carry out his evil schemes against those God loves.

But could our capacity to walk in Christ's authority at least minimize the amount of suffering that takes place on the earth? With all my heart, I believe so. I have to wonder how much suffering we could thwart if we as God's people took our places on the wall and stood firm against the enemy's schemes. Can we honestly say that all hands are currently on deck? I don't think so.

It's been said that there's enough wealth in the world today to wipe out poverty completely. What if we as Christians led the way and gave sacrificially to ministries that provide for the poor? Maybe you're thinking, *I already do that.* But did you know that approximately 95 percent of Christians don't give anything to their local churches or parachurch ministries?

What if every Christian rose up and got serious about the times, their God-given call, and their capacity to make a significant difference in the world? Imagine billions of lights dispelling the darkness, shining ever brighter until the full light of day! Every enemy scheme thwarted is a win for the kingdom. We are ambassadors of heaven appealing to the people of the earth: Be reconciled to God! He loves you with an everlasting love!

You are a warrior in the making. Ask God to show you your place on the wall. Raise your shield against enemy fire, not just for yourself but for the sake of those in bondage to the enemy's lies. What enemy scheme might fall apart because you dared to stand in the gap and pray? Imagine it: Unborn babies saved. Children protected from evil traffickers. Prodigals finding their way back home.

Find a verse that speaks to your God-given call and that deeply resonates with your heart. Try writing it down. Memorize it. Start praying with the boldness and authority entrusted to you.

Say YES! What about the weapons of our warfare? Think of the wars that have ended and the evil schemes intercepted because there

What enemy scheme might fall apart because you **dared** to **stand** in the gap and **pray**?

were discerning, listening Christians who responded to the Lord's call to stand in the gap, who prayed even though it cost them, and who, by their faith, put a stop to the enemy's schemes. Our God-given power and authority allow us to turn the tables on the enemy. We're empowered to interrupt his evil plans. How? By our bold, faith-filled prayers, our others-focused love, and our sacrificial lives lived for the glory of God.

Consider your current battle and get a vision for what *overwhelming victory* might look like for you (see Romans 8:37). Write down a corresponding verse that speaks to the promise of a great victory in your very area of struggle. Then write it out in a paraphrased declaration. Here's an example:

> For God says, "I will break the strength of the wicked,
> but I will increase the power of the godly."
>
> Psalm 75:10

Paraphrased Declaration:

> Mighty Warrior, Father in heaven, blessed be Your name!
> Your kingdom come. Your will be done on earth as it is
> in heaven. I know it's true: You will cut off the strength
> of the wicked and increase the power of the godly!

Personalized Prayer

Mighty King,

I bow before You this day, and honor You. What a treasured gift it is to be a part of Your coming kingdom! Forgive me for the times I've abdicated my responsibility or shrugged my shoulders when You wanted me to stand in the gap for the sake of the kingdom. People pay when I lose my way. Help me bow low today and take my place, to pray and walk and live in my God-given authority. I declare in Jesus' mighty name that I will not only prevail in my personal battles, but I will also help win victory for others. Fill me afresh with Your powerful, potent Holy Spirit. In Jesus' name, I pray. Amen.

Spiritual Intelligence Training
GOD'S WILL, GOD'S WAY

1. God had established Joshua as a great leader among the people (Joshua 3:7). He was a man of sincere faith and high integrity. Let's jump ahead to Joshua 5:13–15. Notice two things about the encounter in this passage: Joshua's bravery in the way he steps up (before he knew who the angel was), and his humility and reverence in the way he bows down. He would need all three for the task ahead of him. We'll look at this exchange more closely in the next chapter, but for now, answer the following questions:
   a. In what ways has God made you brave? In what ways is He asking you for more courage?
   b. Why are humility and reverence before God so vital before heading into battle?
2. Look up the following verses and write down your thoughts: Proverbs 9:10; Proverbs 16:18; 1 Peter 5:6–7; James 4:10.
3. Think back to when the ten spies had scoped out their Promised Land and returned with a bad report because they feared their enemy. Now look at Joshua 6:1 and consider how the tables had turned. Why were the people of Jericho so terrified of the Israelites? They lived in a practically impenetrable city! Write down your thoughts.
4. Read Joshua 6:1–14. Notice God's present-tense declaration in verse 2: "I have given you Jericho."
   a. Look up the following verses and consider some of the things God has already provided for you: Psalm 103:1–5; Luke 10:19; John 10:10; Romans 8:32, 37; 1 Corinthians 2:12; 2 Peter 1:2; and 2 Timothy 1:7. God *has already given you* everything you need. Write out a paraphrased declaration about what you now possess because you are in Christ Jesus.
   b. Imagine the holy anticipation as the Israelites marched silently around the city, only to head back to camp for the night. They weren't allowed to utter a single word. Six days in a row, they

marched in silence. Did some quietly question Joshua's leadership? Were most of them determined not to repeat the mistakes of their parents and grandparents? Did they believe God had *already* given them the victory? Put yourself in their shoes. What emotions would likely surface for you? Write down your thoughts.

5. God told Joshua ahead of time what He was about to do. Joshua trusted God to keep His word and moved forward in faith. Read Joshua 6:15–20 and try to imagine this earth-shattering victory. They say that the walls of Jericho were about twenty-five feet high and twenty feet thick. Yet look what God did! Some scholars believe that the walls fell inward, creating ramps into the city. What if your impossible situation becomes the very thing that provides a way into your promised land? Do you believe it's possible? Write down your thoughts.

6. Intense battles often keep us deeply dependent on God (a good thing). And sometimes, after a sound victory, we forget that God was the One who delivered the victory. We loosen our grip and sometimes even our standards. Read Joshua 7:1–13 and consider the following points:

   a. One man's disobedience weakened the whole community. List four or five consequences of Achan's sin.

   b. Maybe Joshua assumed that since this was a more minor battle than he was used to fighting, he didn't need to consult God. The result? The tide turned against the Israelites, and their courage melted away. *"I've got this"* is a popular phrase, but it doesn't belong in the Christian's vocabulary. We've got nothing apart from God. We need Him every hour. Consider a time when you moved forward without consulting God. What did you learn?

7. Seeking God first takes time and humility. Relying on Him every step of the way calls for teachability. Yet if we hope to see the kind of otherworldly victories God wants to bring us, we must be satisfied with living a humble, dependent life. In what parts of your story do you need to seek God and more proactively listen for His voice? Write down your thoughts.

THREE

Whose Side Are You On?

Stay Teachable

―――

Our goal . . . is not to become powerful but to become holy with Christ's presence. *God promises to empower that which He first makes holy.* Do you want your Christianity to work? Then seek Jesus Himself as your standard of holiness. . . . A mature Christian will be both holy and powerful, but holiness will precede power.[1]

When Joshua was near the town of Jericho, he looked up and saw a man standing in front of him with sword in hand. Joshua went up to him and demanded, "Are you friend or foe?"

"Neither one," he replied. "I am the commander of the Lord's army."

At this, Joshua fell with his face to the ground in reverence. "I am at your command," Joshua said. "What do you want your servant to do?"

The commander of the Lord's army replied, "Take off your sandals, for the place where you are standing is holy." And Joshua did as he was told.

Joshua 5:13–15

God had just told Joshua to be strong and courageous, not to fear or fret. Why? Because the Lord was on Joshua's side! If God is for you, who can stand against you? So why didn't this commander also tell Joshua, "I'm a friend; I'm on your side"?

It's one thing to put your unwavering trust in the Lord; it's another to presume upon God. Though Joshua's heart was all in, the Israelites still had wandering hearts. I've heard some use this story as a claim to neutrality, a reason not to get involved in a particular conflict. But that's not at all the point of this passage. If you read the full story, you'll find that some of God's chosen people had idols in their tents. Their lack of reverence before God made them easy targets for their enemy. The angel reminded Joshua that although God is with us, *we're the ones on God's side*. He sets the terms. He guides our way. He gets the say. When we fail, He loves us still. When we're unfaithful, He remains faithful. But sometimes we need a spiritual reset—a reminder of just who it is that we serve. He is the God of Angel Armies, and we should take Him seriously.[2]

When our kids were young, we'd sit around the dinner table, throw out pop questions, and ask for quick answers. We wanted our sons to learn to think deeply about important topics so that their instinctive reactions reflected cultivated wisdom. We asked, for example, "What's the difference between a good friend and a godly friend?" We loved this question because we wanted our kids to have both kinds of friends, intentionally. Godly friends owned their faith and lived with conviction, and they called our boys higher in their walk of faith (which, of course, also made them good friends). The good friends we referred to described kids who were good, but who didn't know Jesus. We wanted our sons to have unsaved friends to walk with and hopefully influence in a good way. We challenged them constantly to be honest with themselves about who was influencing whom.

Another question we asked one day was, "What's more important, loyalty or integrity?" That was sort of a trick question, and we thoroughly enjoyed watching our boys whisper back and forth, trying to come up with the correct answer. Finally, Jake looked up and said, "We have our answer. Loyalty is important because it's a good character trait. But integrity is more important because it will

We're the ones on **God's side**. He sets the terms. He **guides** our way. He gets the **say**.

keep you on the right path. If you have integrity, you'll be loyal to the right causes." We were impressed!

I often wince when I hear leaders demand loyalty first and foremost. This creates unwritten rules that hinder achievement of the best leadership and outcomes: When someone questions the leader, they're disloyal. If they disagree, they're unfaithful. When they see things from a different perspective, they're out of line. Such judgments of loyalty are counterproductive because checks and balances in leadership are necessary to provide a safety net for all.

Imagine if the leader said, "I want each of us to walk in such a high fear of God and such a deep pursuit of holiness that our lives continually bear the fruit of the Spirit. I want to create an atmosphere for growth where we all have an open-door policy. If you see something in me or I see something in you, let's talk about it so we can grow in the grace and knowledge of God. Pride is our enemy. Humility and honor before God and each other will keep us all grounded. We must humbly submit to God's authority, or we'll have no authority in ministry."

God perpetually distances Himself from the proud and draws near to and empowers the humble. Picture it in your mind: Imagine the God of the universe pulling back or drawing near based on the posture of one's heart. He is ever-present—omnipresent—but His supernatural empowering presence falls on those who fear Him. Every day, countless Christians grieve the Spirit or walk by the Spirit, both of which create ripples of destruction or redemption, respectively, on the earth. That's why Scripture implores us to guard our hearts with all diligence, for out of our heart spring the issues of life (see Proverbs 4:23).

Though we make much of so many other sins, pride is the worst of all evils because it exalts itself above the knowledge of God. Picture two scenarios with me: The celebrity pastor, hanging out in the green room with assistants at his beck and call. He has built a ginormous ministry, and many people idolize him. (He loves all of the accommodations that come with his position, and he'd never say it out loud, but he's pretty sure God is as impressed with him as he is with himself.) Several miles down the road sits the local prison. A convicted felon kneels on the concrete floor. He grabs fistfuls of his bedsheet and puts his forehead on the bed. He cries out for mercy and begs Jesus to forgive him, cleanse him, and come into his life as Savior and Lord.

Who do you suppose Jesus moved toward at that moment?

> The high and lofty one who lives in eternity,
>   the Holy One, says this:
> "I live in the high and holy place
>   with those whose spirits are contrite and humble.
> I restore the crushed spirit of the humble
>   and revive the courage of those with repentant hearts."
>
> Isaiah 57:15

Just because God is with us and for us doesn't mean *we're* always on the Lord's side. He's on the side of faith, hope, love. He's on the side of forgiveness, redemption, and restoration. He's on the side of humility, brokenness, and compassion. He's on the side of the moment-by-moment obedience that is the Spirit-led life.

We make dangerous assumptions when we assume that because God is for us, He also endorses everything we do. He wouldn't be God if He could turn a blind eye to attitudes and actions that are in direct conflict with who He is.

God knows our hearts, and He notices departures in us before we catch them in ourselves. Picture modern-day believers traveling en masse (like the Israelites on their way to their Promised Land). There's a clear path of power in the center of God's will. It's where we gain discernment, walk in our God-assigned influence, and cultivate an ever-deepening love for Jesus and for the way that He walked. It's the path of peace, power, and purity. It's the path of boldness, courage, and strength. It's the path of sacrificial love and mountain-moving faith.

Now picture some of your fellow travelers venturing off God's best path for them. They distance themselves from the pack to make their own way. They're having a great time but have lost their sensitivity to the Spirit, lost sight of the very reason they're on this journey. By wandering from the rest, they've thinned the crowd of those on the battlefield. Consumed with this world's cares, they live like worldly civilians and not like the kingdom soldiers they are (see 2 Timothy 2:4).

Read John's words to his *fellow believers*:

Do not love this world nor the things it offers you, for when you love the world, you do not have the love of the Father in you. For the world offers only a craving for physical pleasure, a craving for everything we see, and pride in our achievements and possessions. These are not from the Father, but are from this world. And this world is fading away, along with everything that people crave. But anyone who does what pleases God will live forever.

1 John 2:15–17

The problem with the wandering path is that it's heavily populated. The path of obedience is often a lonely one. When one wanders, others follow. When enough professing Christ-followers take the worldly way instead of the godly way, the Spirit is grieved, the enemy rejoices, and the world receives a mixed message about the power of the resurrection. Moreover, when citizens of the kingdom abdicate their God-given sphere of influence, it creates a vacuum for the enemy's influence to fill, at a high cost to the kingdom and the world. Our calling matters that much.

Not to say there's no room for feasting, fun, and celebration on the path of obedience. We must learn how to enjoy our journey! We'll talk about that more in the next chapter. But I think we all know the difference between a thank offering of celebration and an indulgent lifestyle. One nourishes us. The other slows our progress and dims our witness.

The problem with the **wandering** path is that it's heavily populated. The path of **obedience** is often a lonely one.

Here's another way to look at it. Jesus is on one side of the battle (the right side), and Satan is on the other. Jesus regularly intercedes for us (and others). The narrow road of obedience compels us to see people—made in God's image—from a redemptive perspective. Because that's what Jesus has done for us.

The broad road is paved with self-righteousness and pride. We didn't save ourselves, yet somehow we feel others should save themselves. We think nothing of nailing our list to the cross and holding someone else's list in our hand.[3] Where did we learn such a thing?

Satan regularly accuses us (and others). He spews accusations all day long. We take the bait without even realizing it. People behave in unrighteous ways. Some live with constant chaos and can never seem to get a handle on things; Christians openly indulge in sin and justify it; leaders say one thing and do another . . . we're faced with countless opportunities to make assessments and sum up situations. But when we step in as judge, jury, and accuser, we cross over the battle line and join our voice with the enemy's rants.

When we humble ourselves before God and, out of love and reverence before Him, forgive a deeply painful offense, we're on the Lord's side. When we trust God to vindicate and heal us, we stand in power with our King.

When we make light of obedience and simply do our own thing because we think God's grace covers us, we trample Christ's precious sacrifice. And we abandon our post. Listen to Jesus' sobering words to us:

> Anyone who isn't with me opposes me, and anyone who isn't working with me is actually working against me.
>
> Matthew 12:30

Satan:	Jesus:
Accuser, Confuser	Advocate, Prince of Peace
Pride, Condemnation	Humility, Intercession
Disobedience, Independence	Obedience, Submission to the Father

Satan:	Jesus:
Disregard for God's ways	Reverence before the Father
Ungrateful, Entitled	Grateful, Generous
Bitter, Unforgiving	Joyful, Compassionate
Gluttony, Overconsumption	Moderation, Restraint, Fasting
Consumer, Self-Justified	Sacrificial, Inconvenient Love

I know this isn't a popular message in a world of entitlement, where we endorse and validate "my truth" and "your truth." But this is God's truth, and we must heed it if we're going to thrive and win on the battlefield in the days ahead. Read Paul's sobering words from the book of Romans:

> Those who are dominated by the sinful nature think about sinful things, but those who are controlled by the Holy Spirit think about things that please the Spirit. So letting your sinful nature control your mind leads to death. But letting the Spirit control your mind leads to life and peace.
>
> Romans 8:5–6

I believe that the days of carnal Christianity are officially over. The battle is heating up. The middle of the road will soon disappear and everyone will have to choose sides. Am I on the Lord's side or the world's?

> Loving God means keeping his commandments, and his commandments are not burdensome. For every child of God defeats this evil world, and we achieve this victory through our faith. And who can win this battle against the world? Only those who believe that Jesus is the Son of God.
>
> 1 John 5:3–5

In the days ahead, you'll see a clear distinction between those who fear God and those who don't. It's time now to rend not our garments, but our hearts[4] and to seek the Lord while He may be found.

We're not going to do it all right all the time. We'll get it wrong every single day. Thankfully, God's not asking for perfection, but He is calling us to a purity of heart. With all of my heart, I believe we're coming into a day when we will see God move in ways we never dreamed possible. I also tend to think this will be a great and terrible time of deliverance and discipline, purifying and empowering. It's wise for us to humble ourselves now and give God full access to our stories and our character so that He might reveal the nuanced ways we depart from His best for us, ways that we cannot at this moment discern.

God's Power through Us

It's a sobering thought that just because God uses all kinds of people and situations, it doesn't mean He endorses their lives. You'll notice that in the Old Testament He used wicked kings, foreign nations, and even a donkey to accomplish His purposes. If God is going to do what He's going to do, why does it matter whether or not we're wholly devoted to Him?

Well, for several reasons. For one, He deserves our highest praise and our best offerings. Paul charged us in the book of Romans to offer our bodies as a living sacrifice, holy and acceptable to Him! (See Romans 12:1.) He further said, "You are not your own; you've been bought with a price. So glorify God in your bodies" (1 Corinthians 6:19–20, my paraphrase). Second, our call to consecrate ourselves before God that we might be used by Him on the earth today is actually a mandate, and one that's so often overlooked by many.

If you keep yourself pure, you will be a special utensil for honorable use. Your life will be clean, and you will be ready for the Master to use you for every good work.

Run from anything that stimulates youthful lusts. Instead, pursue righteous living, faithfulness, love, and peace. Enjoy the companionship of those who call on the Lord with pure hearts.

2 Timothy 2:21–22

Third, the reason we enter into a deep, abiding relationship with Jesus—living as He lived and doing what He would do—is because of the price He paid for us. He said (and showed) that we were worth dying for. Well, He's worth living for, wouldn't you say? He purchased our freedom with His precious blood and grafted us into His royal family. Our identity is forever changed and secure. With identity comes privilege. And with privilege comes responsibility.

Don't you want to partner with God to see the miraculous come to earth? For years, I've prayed that the sick would recover, the depressed would be delivered, the rejected would know they are accepted, the lost would be found, and the righteous would be mobilized into their God-sized calling. I'm not satisfied with vanilla Christianity. And the world is desperate to know and experience the miraculous, life-changing power of the gospel, even if they don't know it yet.

In case you need some fresh reminders of God's willingness and ability to intervene in the lives of His people, consider these:

- Moses (a man humbly and wholly submitted to God) miraculously led the Israelites out of slavery. Think about the many miracles God performed along the way. (See Exodus 14.)
- Joseph (a man humbly and wholly submitted to God) was miraculously delivered from prison and placed in the palace to help save a nation. (See Genesis 37–50.)
- Daniel (a man humbly and wholly submitted to God) stayed committed to the Lord in a godless culture, and God elevated him to an essential level of leadership and influence. (See the book of Daniel.)

- Ruth (an outsider, a Moabite woman, humbly and wholly submitted to God) left her homeland to follow a God she could not see but knew in her heart, and God grafted her into the lineage of our Savior. (See the book of Ruth.)
- Peter (a hasty, self-striving man, humbled, redeemed, and restored) was used by God as a key leader in establishing the early church. (See Acts 3.)
- Paul (a terrorist and persecutor of Christians turned radical follower of Christ) turned the world upside down with his bold faith, and God gave us much of the New Testament through him. (See Acts 9.)

There's truly no limit to what God will do through a life humbly, wholly devoted to Him. He's looking for saints today who are willing to rise this hour and believe Him to be the God He declares Himself to be! When God searches the world over to find faith in the hearts of men, may He find holy, humble, powerful faith in us.

Prayerful Reflective Questions

1. *Father in heaven, have I, in any way, wandered from Your best path for me? Show me my heart.*
2. *Have I, in my assessments of others, crossed over to the side of the accuser? Help me see things from Your point of view. I want to intercede with power!*
3. *What thought patterns repeatedly lead me astray? Please give me a new song to sing, faith declarations that strengthen my stance.*
4. *Father, in what ways have I limited Your power in my life? Grant me a vision for what miracle-working power might look like in my life.*

The Humble Way: Following Jesus on His terms is serious business, but He never wants us to walk on eggshells or continually brace for impact. He wants us to know how to rest in His care, to be joyful and confident in His love, and to cultivate such intimacy with the Holy Spirit that we notice the slightest wince of the Holy Spirit within us.

The less we trust ourselves, the more we trust God.

The more we decrease, the more He increases. If we want to walk in God's power, we must become increasingly acquainted with and rooted in His tender love for His people. If you wonder if you've wandered, just look at the fruit. Are you feeling irritated, judgmental? Are you tempted to construct a case against someone because you're anticipating an argument? Or are you growing in the grace and knowledge of Jesus? Are you putting a higher priority on the peace of God? Are you becoming more and more convinced that the Savior not only goes before you, but He's got your back too (see Psalm 139:5)?

The more often we return to our First Love, the more we'll be able to impart that love to a world so desperately in need. Furthermore, knowing and walking in the intense love of God is one of our highest forms of spiritual warfare. Demons tremble when we operate in Holy Spirit–inspired love.

Here's a passage to prayerfully ponder in humility and with receptivity:

> When I think of all this, I fall to my knees and pray to the Father, the Creator of everything in heaven and on earth. I pray that from his glorious, unlimited resources he will empower you with inner strength through his Spirit. Then Christ will make his home in your hearts as you trust in him. Your roots will grow down into God's

love and keep you strong. And may you have the power to understand, as all God's people should, how wide, how long, how high, and how deep his love is. May you experience the love of Christ, though it is too great to understand fully. Then you will be made complete with all the fullness of life and power that comes from God.

Ephesians 3:14–19

Discern the Fiery Arrows: Jesus said that unless we're gathering with Him (drawing people to Him and His Gospel-saving message), we're actually scattering the flock. Sobering, no? We must know that the enemy is so fiercely opposed to our call that he'll stop at nothing to distract us from it. Sometimes the fiery arrows come in the way of worldly pursuits, distractions, and self-justified attitudes. When we're distracted by such things, we miss the Savior's work in our midst.

Discern the arrows and write them down; see them for what they are. You have one enemy, and he attacks in often predictable ways. But we're not going to put up with it any longer.

Say NO! We have more grit and gumption to say no when we know what we're saying yes to. May God grant you a vision for the great work He's called you to and the amazing power He promises you as you walk in His way. Picture the days ahead. There will be a clear distinction between those who walk in holy power and those who don't. Ask the Lord to make you wise to the enemy's predictable schemes against you. Use your shield like you mean it.

Find a verse that speaks to your God-given call and that profoundly resonates with your heart. Try writing it down. Memorize it. Start praying with the boldness and authority entrusted to you.

Say YES! What's the deep desire rising within you this hour? Prodigals coming home? Revival springing up in your city? That the Church might awaken this hour? God has anointed and appointed you for this hour. Pay attention to what He stirs up within you. Discern whom He's called you to pray for and go after it with a newfound boldness, humility, and courage. Refuse to cross over to the wrong side of the battle. You are a part of the conquering army of God!

73

Consider your current battle and get a vision for what *overwhelming victory* might look like for you (see Romans 8:37). Write down a corresponding verse that speaks to the promise of a great victory in your very area of struggle. Then write it out in a paraphrased declaration. Here's an example:

Therefore, since we are surrounded by such a huge crowd of witnesses to the life of faith, let us strip off every weight that slows us down, especially the sin that so easily trips us up. And let us run with endurance the race God has set before us.

Hebrews 12:1

Paraphrased Declaration:

Mighty Warrior, Father in heaven, I am all in! I will run
with purpose, pray with power, and walk in the authority
You've entrusted to me. I won't fall back, fall out, or
give up. I will run with endurance and active persistence,
knowing You empower me every step of the way. Thanks
be to God, who always leads me in triumph!

Personalized Prayer

*Jesus, I surrender to You, to Your lordship, Your kingship, and
Your rule and reign in my life. On my own, I have no power*

to save anyone, to change anyone. But in You and with You, I can walk in a power that sets me free. Forgive me for so often wandering off Your highest and best path for me. Heighten my sensitivity to Your Spirit. Awaken new life in me! May Your kingdom power flow mightily in and through me. I want more of You! In Your precious name, I pray. Amen.

Spiritual Intelligence Training
DO YOU KNOW WHO YOU ARE?

1. The Israelites asked for a king, and though this request displeased God, He answered their prayers and chose Saul to step into that role. From the beginning, Saul battled feelings of inferiority, selfishness, and insecurity. Read Saul's response to Samuel's proclamation that he'd be the next king (1 Samuel 9:19–21). From your perspective, what's the difference between humility and insecurity?

2. Read 1 Samuel 10:6–9 and ponder God's promise to Saul as we work our way through the following questions.

3. First, God let Saul know that he would be king and that God's power would be with him. Then God announced it to the people. Read 1 Samuel 10:17–23 and make a note of Saul's instinctive reaction to the announcement. Why do you suppose Saul hid in the baggage?

   a. Pause here for a moment and answer this question as honestly and thoughtfully as possible. Are there promises God has made you, assurances He has given you that you've passed over, disregarded, or forgotten about altogether? Write down your thoughts. God wants you to bring those to the forefront of your mind and ponder them once again.

4. Read 1 Samuel 13:1–13 and consider this: Sometimes God uses delays to test our faith and our willingness to obey Him above all else. It's easy to skim over this passage and give Saul a pass for his actions. But obviously, neither God nor Samuel viewed Saul's actions as reasonable or understandable. Identify Saul's *actions, excuses,* and *attitudes* and write them down.

5. Read 1 Samuel 14 and answer the following questions.

   a. Jonathan possessed faith, courage, and wisdom. In what ways do you see him displaying these three virtues in this chapter?

   b. Saul, in the meantime, became blind to his sin and unwisely reactionary to the circumstances. He sought God as a last resort, not as the first order of business. In what ways do you see Saul behaving in ways beneath him as a father and a king?

   c. My NLT Bible's study note offers this great insight: "Like a leaf tossed about by the wind, Saul vacillated between his feelings and his convictions. Everything he said and did was selfish because he worried about himself. . . . *Although Saul had been called by God and had a mission in life,* he struggled constantly with jealousy, insecurity, arrogance, impulsiveness, deceit. He did not decide to be wholeheartedly committed to God. *Because Saul would not let God's love give rest to his heart, he never became God's man.*"[5] It's shocking how Saul sabotaged his God-given calling. But I wonder how much we miss because we look inward more than upward. Write down your thoughts.

6. Let's take one more look at Saul's slippery ways. Read 1 Samuel 15:1–30 and answer the following questions:

   a. In this passage, we see Saul's acts of disobedience, pride, and blame. Identify these in the story.

   b. In 1 Samuel 15:17–18, you can almost hear Samuel's impassioned plea to Saul, "Although you may think little of yourself, are you not the leader of the tribes of Israel? The LORD has anointed you . . . sent you on a mission." If Samuel were to grab you by the shoulders today, look you in the eye, and issue an impassioned plea, what do you think he'd say to you?

7. In verse 22, Samuel asks, in other words, "What's more important: your sacrifices or your obedience to God's voice?" Sometimes we hide in our church busyness, and we miss the more significant work God wants to do in and through us. And obedience to His voice sometimes calls for the step of faith to believe that what He says about us is true. What does God say about you? Do you know who you are? Write down your thoughts and boldly and humbly *share them with a friend.*

FOUR

Wisdom in the Off-Season

Stay Strong

In a world that relentlessly reduces us to skin and bones, our God speaks abundant, outrageous life. He creates. He renovates. He turns trash into treasure, fish into a feast, and a nearly invisible grain of faith into a mountain-moving force. He speaks, and beauty grows wild on our battlefield, causing giants to fall and joy to rise. He moves, and hope runs loose through broken dreams, breathing life where death once danced. He is the God of more-than-enough. Believe it.[1]

I feel as though I'm writing this book in the middle of a hailstorm. Lyme disease has been my foe for over thirty years. Sometimes it seems I have the upper hand, and other times, not so much. Right now, I'm in the middle of a surge of inflammation and neurological symptoms that make it difficult to focus, spell, and write coherently. Yet overriding the struggle is God's nearness and His grace. *Keep on keeping on,* He says. And so I do.

As I mentioned in a previous chapter, whenever I'm in the middle of a battle, I first discern the "why" behind it, and then I take my stand based on what I know to be true. For better and sometimes for worse, the struggle changes us. It doesn't matter if you continually face a predictable foe (e.g., struggles in marriage, health, finances, etc.) or if a new trial hits you out of nowhere, opposition impacts you. Standing in faith for long stretches can take a toll on the soul. It can also energize you, depending on how you frame the difficult and disappointing parts of your battle. When we fight the good fight of faith, we can get a little battered and, at the same time, beautified. Though we endure our blows from the enemy, our trials are achieving something in us we cannot comprehend.

Because God is well aware of our heart's condition, He takes us out of the intense fight from time to time. We're still soldiers in the Lord's army, still alert to enemy schemes, but we're pulled from the front lines and brought back to base camp, where we can recover, get a good meal, repair our weapons, and get out of fight/flight mode.

When God pulls me back from the front lines, one of the first things I like to do is take inventory. Why? Because the battle has changed me. I know some things now that I didn't know before. And I want to remember those things. I've realized that it's possible to come out of a war with a firmer grasp on some truths and utterly disillusioned or deceived about others. Trauma has a way of impacting our theology—sometimes for good, but not always.

I've seen folks come out of trauma with an unbiblical theology, disconnected from God, holding to a form of religion that is void of power. They decide that the Bible is just a book of inspiring stories, not God's inerrant Word. They may lean more toward intellectual and philosophical pursuits instead of spending time in God's Word, enjoying His presence. They've decided that He's not an involved Father but more of a hands-off God. It's heartbreaking.

Thankfully, I've also seen Pharisaical Christians walk through suffering and come out the other side with tenderness and compassion that are absolutely stunning. I've seen godly men and women walk through the valley of the shadow and emerge heroes. They come out

How do we know
if our battles have
served us well?
We will **emerge**
from them leaning
on the arm of our
Beloved.

with dirt on their faces, grit in their hearts, and anointing on their lives. I want every one of my battles to serve me that way.

How do we know if our battles have served us well? We will emerge from them leaning on the arm of our Beloved. We will find that through our suffering, Jesus has deposited within us new levels of humility, compassion, and love, and we

- are a little wiser to the enemy's schemes;
- take ourselves less seriously and God more seriously;
- know, on a deeper level, how to maintain joy and peace in our hearts; and
- find ourselves less attached to the things of this earth and more passionate about eternity with Jesus, and all that implies.

We know our trials have served us well when we come through with a greater desire to worship God for who and how He is, and we know that our safest place is in the center of His will.

We can rejoice, too, when we run into problems and trials, for we know that they help us develop endurance. And endurance develops strength of character, and character strengthens our confident hope of salvation. And this hope will not lead to disappointment. For we know how dearly God loves us, because he has given us the Holy Spirit to fill our hearts with his love.

Romans 5:3–5

That is why we never give up. Though our bodies are dying, our spirits are being renewed every day. For our present troubles are small and won't last very long. Yet they produce for us a glory that vastly outweighs them and will last forever! So we don't look at the troubles we can see now; rather, we fix our gaze on things that cannot be seen. For the things we see now will soon be gone, but the things we cannot see will last forever.[2]

2 Corinthians 4:16–18

Questions to Ask Ourselves

1. *What do I know about God now that I didn't know prior to this trial?*

2. *How has this battle impacted my theology?* Have I adjusted my theology in any way, manipulated my faith to match my life? (An excellent way to discern this is to note if there are lingering disappointments in God or in others, offenses over unresolved pain, unhealthy indulgences that you justify because of what you had to walk through, or a biblical compromise you know you're making because it feels too painful or difficult to stay aligned with God's Word.)

3. *How has my battle impacted my perspective of others?* (Ideally, our battles refine us in such a way that we grow in love and compassion for others, but if we don't process our hardships in a redemptive way, we'll find ourselves irritated with others, impatient with their weaknesses, and dismissive of their trials because they don't compare to all we've endured.)

4. *What biblical truths did I forget that I need to remember?* And what truths did I remember that I don't want to forget? (This is a hugely important exercise, one that's well worth your time.)

5. *What were the defining moments of my battle, when the storm raged and God met me there?* (This is your story, your song. This is part of your amazing testimony; you are an overcomer.)

6. *What in me still needs healing?* (It's time to assess the damages. God is deeply committed to restoring you in whatever ways you need. Do you believe it?)

7. *How am I better because of this battle?* What has this trial done *for* you, *in* you, and *through* you? In what ways has this opposition served you well?

How we view our **trials** when we're in them and what we tell ourselves about them on the other side **directly** impacts the kind of **warrior** we become.

Taking inventory after a battle will make you a better warrior. It is wise to do this during the off-season because it helps you know how to recover, and it enables you see the ground you've gained because of the fight.

How we view our trials when we're in them and what we tell ourselves about them on the other side directly impacts the kind of warrior we become. We'll become wishy-washy soldiers if our belief in God's goodness is always up for grabs, or if we think it's all up to us, or if we assume God owes us a different kind of life than the one we're living. Some things we need to settle in our hearts, sooner rather than later.

My friend Tessa Afshar is a brilliant novelist. In her book *Jewel of the Nile*, one of her characters writes a poem, "Angel Scars," to help process battle scars. This excerpt is voiced by an angel he encounters:

> "You have salvation; indeed, you have life.
> But has God saved you from even worse strife?
> Recalling that day, won't you weep and fear?
> Is this scar not a sign you'll lose all you hold dear?
>
> "How strange," he said, "is the memory of your heart.
> You retain all darkness—but with grace, you part.
> The threats of yesteryear cast shadows on the morrow
> until fear becomes your tomb, and joy is consumed by
>   sorrow.
>
> "You cannot see the Hand that saved you before
> has yet more love and grace, more strength in store.
> Your scars don't point only to the enemy's power.
> Much more are they reminders that God is your strong
>   tower.
> He did love you then, and treasures you still;
> one day your soul will know this; it will drink its fill.

"With every hideous pain, you fear much more;
But we angels know suffering as a holy door.

"The road that leads to valleys will in the end impart,
God's hope and his glory; the start of a new heart."[3]

Read this excerpt a few more times. It's so insightful. We know we need some Fatherly attention when one of our takeaways from battle is, *If God allowed this to happen, what worse fate awaits me?* Instead of marveling at His faithfulness, we shrink back in mistrust. If that's you, there's no condemnation, but there *is* an invitation. It's an appeal to heal. Are you ready to open up the basement of your soul and address the things you've stuffed down there during your recent battle? God will help you.[4]

Several years ago, author and pastor Jeff Manion said something on my radio show that I've never forgotten: *"We try to become experts at not getting hurt. We need to become experts at learning to heal."*[5]

As the poem we read says, our heart's memory is strange—what imprints on our soul, and the things we so easily forget. If left to our instincts, we'll hold on to our trauma and bury the beautiful memories that could play a part in our healing.

Sooner or later every believer discovers that the Christian life is a battleground, not a playground.[6]

It's important to remember that God is the One who decides when our battle is over, not us. If you recall from Scripture, when most kings were going out to war, David stayed behind in Jerusalem. King David sent someone to fight in his place while he retreated to the roof of his palace. Just because he had won some valiant victories in the past didn't mean he had earned the sweat equity to opt out of his present battles.

86

God decides when we rest and when we war. Not us. His ways are higher than our ways. He knows that when our flesh is weak, the smartest thing we can do is engage our faith muscles. I shudder to think of who I'd be and the choices I'd have made if not for some of the intense battles that kept me diligently engaged with God's Word. David's decision to abdicate his responsibility set in motion a series of tragic events (see 2 Samuel 11).

Then there's Joshua. God instructed Joshua to occupy the land of Canaan, and it took him about seven years of intense warfare to carry out God's plan. Then God gave Joshua and the people rest from battle (see Joshua 21:44).

There will be when times you want to retreat and God says run, and other times when you'll want to run and God will tell you to stay put and watch Him work. There are several things we can learn from all the battles recorded in the Old Testament. Here are a few: *Our emotions are not always wise counselors. Our perception of our strength or lack thereof is usually wrong, so we need to get our marching orders from God alone. We don't stand a chance in battle unless God has led us to it. We can trust Him to come through for us when we're out of strength and overwhelmed. We serve the God of the breakthrough, and one way or another, His purposes will prevail.*

Advice for the Off-Season

Here are some practical ways you can steward your off-season. The goal is to get your strength back, to keep your heart and your faith engaged, and to heal in the ways you need to heal.

- Take your worship to a whole new level. (That may be a bit uncomfortable, depending on your denominational background, but there's a biblical basis for it.) See Psalm 84:2.
- Expand your study and time in God's Word. Memorize new passages of Scripture and pray them often.

- Reengage in your faith community if you've become isolated.
- Be careful not to disengage or drop your guard. Your enemy is constantly looking for an opportunity to steal from you. Don't give him one.
- Consider the weapons of your warfare (Ephesians 6:13–17), and each day recognize their importance and function in your life (shoes of peace, belt of truth, breastplate of righteousness, helmet of salvation, shield of faith, sword of the Spirit). Since our victory in the battle directly correlates to our use of these weapons, we're wise to familiarize ourselves with them when we're not in the heat of the fight. Put on your armor daily.
- Pray for your fellow believers who are right now in the heat of the battle. God didn't design us to do this alone.
- See a Christian counselor if necessary. Sort through what you've just come through until you're more encouraged by the fruit of your suffering than you are afraid of a future trial.
- Spend some time dwelling on your good memories, ones that ignite joy. Sit with them and linger there. Studies show this is nourishing for your brain, your cells, and your soul. You'll be amazed at how this exercise will refresh your perspective.
- Have fun! Add laughter back to your days. Celebrate your victories. Make plans with friends or family and be fully present with them.

Prayerful Reflective Questions

1. *Heavenly Father, how have my battles negatively impacted me?*
2. *Lord Jesus, what in me still needs to heal?*
3. *In what ways have my trials served me well?*

4. *Lord, please speak to me: Is there a discipline I need to add and/or an indulgence I need to stop so that I'm better prepared for my next battle?*

The Humble Way: As Roy Hession advises us in *When I Saw Him,*

> We ought not be living the up-and-down life, but we should be living the down-and-up life! Down to the cross in repentance and up again through the power of His blood, in praise to God; down to give in on some new point on which we are convicted and then up again to praise Him for restoration and peace; down to surrender our rights on some matter and up again to have His life living anew in us. And not only in such matters as these are we to know the down-and-up life, but in every other circumstance or difficulty where we are brought low. Phillips translates Paul's phrase in 2 Corinthians 4:9, "struck down, but not destroyed," as "knocked down, but not knocked out." We come up again because we have in us the same life that was in Him.[7]

Anyone who wants tidy faith you can put in a box and wrap up with a bow won't find it following Jesus. It's the narrow path. The radical way. The life-transforming way of the Savior. One moment we're okay, and the next, we misstep or stumble. And that's okay. That's why we need community, honesty, safety within godly relationships, and grace for ourselves, for it's what God has poured out on us.

Humbly and prayerfully meditate on this passage until it seeps into your soul:

> Yet it was our weaknesses he carried;
>   it was our sorrows that weighed him down.
> And we thought his troubles were a punishment from God,
>   a punishment for his own sins!

But he was pierced for our rebellion,
  crushed for our sins.
He was beaten so we could be whole.
  He was whipped so we could be healed.

Isaiah 53:4–5

Discern the Fiery Arrows: Sometimes after the battle dies down, you realize there are a few arrow tips that found their way into your heart and need to be removed. For example, God removed a poisonous arrow tip from my soul that pierced me with the message that God's promises of protection didn't apply to me—that I would have to endure everything I feared. Whenever we feel like a have-not, or like we're a substandard child of God, we can know there's a poisonous arrow still lodged in us.

Pause and ask God to show you those places in your soul. Identify the incident or circumstance and the enemy's intent behind that experience. Often, we need to separate the person/people from the situation. The memory of offense will continue to injure us until we forgive our offender, remember who our real enemy is, and then do the necessary business with the Lord. Take the condition of your heart seriously. God will reveal, heal, correct, and redirect. Give Him access to those places you'd rather not acknowledge and to those emotions you'd rather not feel. Write out your thoughts, prayers, and insights. In due time, you'll be able to release the person and tell that enemy, *I know what you tried to do here, but you won't get away with it. You don't get to write my story. God does. I refuse your lies and renounce any agreement I've made up to this point. In the name of Jesus, I cancel your scheme against me, and I stand in agreement with what the Lord Jesus says of me!*

Say NO! Even when God occasionally gives us a break from the intense battle, the devil never takes a break. He's just sly enough to attack in ways we don't see coming. We're so used to blocking arrows coming at us from one direction, we're sometimes surprised to face an attack from another angle or front. The temptation during the off-season is to leave the little foxes alone and let them nip at the vine.[8] We figure that since we're not in a significant battle, we don't need to major in the minors. But it's those little nuanced places where the enemy finds access to take what doesn't belong to him. Where are those places for you? Health? Relationships? Spiritual disciplines? Decide now that you're going to guard your heart and guard your yard against enemy influence.

Find a verse that speaks to your God-given call and that profoundly resonates with your heart. Try writing it down. Memorize it. Start praying with the boldness and authority entrusted to you.

Say YES! The off-season is a great time to ask God for a sense about your next place of promise. What dreams is He stirring up in you? Which people in your life still need to be set free? In what ways might He ask you to step out of the boat in the days ahead? Raise your sword, cut through your fears, apathy, or anything else that may hold you back, and create some time and space to wait on the Lord. Give Him your bold, courageous yes.

Consider your current calling and get a vision for what increase, or multiplication, might look like in your life (e.g., helping more people, walking in a more significant measure of kingdom power, giving away more money). Write down a corresponding verse that speaks to the promise of God's ability to work in and through you. Now write it out in a paraphrased declaration. Here's an example:

Now all glory to God, who is able, through his mighty power at work within us, to accomplish infinitely more than we might ask or think. Glory to him in the church and in Christ Jesus through all generations forever and ever! Amen.

Ephesians 3:20–21

Paraphrased Declaration:

In Jesus' name, and by His grace, I am filled with the Spirit of the Living God, who is able to do in and through me above and beyond all I could ever dare to ask or think! So I say YES, Lord! Have Your way in me! Grant me more faith and glorify Your name!

Personalized Prayer

Lord Jesus, I don't know what to say. I don't know what to do. So I bow low and open my hands to You. Thank You, Jesus, for dying my death, for bearing my shame, and for saving my soul through the power of Your name. I worship You. I thank You! And I humble myself before You now. Speak to me, O God. Change me. Renew me. Restore me. And use me in ways totally disproportionate to who I am. Because that's what You do. That's who You are. Oh, how I love You. Thank You for Your intimate presence in my life. Amen.

Spiritual Intelligence Training
STAY HEALTHY, STAY STRONG

1. When King Nebuchadnezzar besieged Jerusalem, he abducted many of the young men from Judah's royal family. He asked only for the strong, healthy, well-versed, and gifted to serve in his royal palace. They were to be trained for three years and would then enter the king's royal service. Read Daniel 1:1–7 and imagine such a jarring turn of events. Put yourself in Daniel's shoes. How do you think he felt? What kinds of thoughts likely ran through his head?

2. Read Daniel 1:8–21 and consider these questions:

   a. God gave the chief of staff both respect and affection for Daniel (v. 9). How might Daniel have behaved to garner such respect and admiration? Use your imagination a little.

   b. Though Daniel was likely wonderful to work with, he knew that his ultimate allegiance belonged to God alone. Thus, he took a significant risk when he asked permission to refrain from eating food deemed unacceptable by his people. Daniel had been brought to Babylon, trained in Babylon, and given a Babylonian name. Yet he never lost sight of his true identity and calling. As my friend Paul Hurckman says, to effectively participate in culture, "we first have to define our non-participation."[9] Where do we draw the line between what God asks of us and what culture easily accepts? What are those lines for you?

3. When we've suffered injustice, it's tempting to throw convictions out the window and indulge in ways we typically wouldn't. Given the depths of injustice Daniel endured, his convictions are all the more admirable. What allowances do you make for yourself that you know you shouldn't?

4. Reread Daniel 1:15–21 and notice two factors at play here. From a physical perspective, Daniel and his men were healthier and mentally

sharper because their diet was clean. From a spiritual standpoint, they made these choices because of their godly convictions, and according to verse 17, God *gifted* them abilities that made them stand out above the rest.

    a. Is there a situation in your life that feels unjust or disappointing?

    b. Might God have you there for a purpose? Write out your thoughts.

    c. Is there a physical discipline God is nudging you toward? Write it down.

    d. Is there a special gift He has imparted to you that you'd love to see Him empower in a new and noticeable way? Explain.

5. Sometimes, during seasons of obscurity, we forget that we're still "on duty." We loosen our grip on the promises of God and drift into mindsets that weaken us. If that's you, what can you do for yourself physically, emotionally, and spiritually to stay in tip-top condition during this season of your life?

6. Read Daniel 2 and contrast Daniel's humble, confident attitude with Saul's mindset (from the last chapter's Spiritual Intelligence Training section). Daniel feared God and was ready to serve Him. What are three or four ways in this story that Daniel exercised wisdom and a pure heart?

7. When you live with conviction, people without conviction will find a reason to find fault, even if you're innocent. Read Daniel 3 and notice, once again, this jarring turn of events. Shadrach, Meshach, and Abednego lived in the palace (for exiles, they had a pretty good gig!), so for them to risk it all for the sake of God's honor was incredible. They didn't acquire this kind of character overnight. They walked the line of serving the king while honoring their King every single day.

    a. Read verses 16–18 again and imagine yourself in a modern-day scenario like this. What would have to change/grow/heal in your life for you to stand with such courage and conviction?

b. Read verses 25–30 again and marvel at God's hand in this situation. Because of their conviction, the king realized he was no match for almighty God, who adequately put the king in his place, and the king then promoted the three young men to serve at a higher level. There's always a cost to following Jesus. How far will you go with Him? What negotiations have you employed or limits have you put on your relationship with God? Write down your thoughts and ask God to help you sort through them.

FIVE

What's Discernment?

Stay Close

Let the mountain of the Lord captivate and allure you to its peaks.
There you will be taught His ways. There you will cry for change,
deep change, change from within that makes you more like God,
change that makes the best you — the you God created you to be.[1]

Y ou're a part of the underground church. You've been discov-
ered and you're going to prison. You have no Bible. Just a pen
and a pad of paper. What do you know about God? What do you
remember about the Bible?" we asked the kids in our youth group.
"Are there worship songs that have imprinted on your soul in a way
that compels you to look beyond your circumstances and trust God?
Write down everything you know so you won't forget it."

Wide-eyed and curious, those kids looked up at us, unsure of
where this was going.

"For the next hour, you're alone in prison," we continued. "Go
find a place to sit away from your friends and write down everything
and anything you know about Jesus and your Christian faith."

What happened next shocked and surprised us. The kids whose
parents had no faith to speak of really owned their faith. They weren't

at all intimidated by the exercise. With their heads down, they wrote furiously, as though they might run out of paper. Others, who were raised in the faith but had much handed to them, looked like they were entirely out of their element. Had they been listening to their parents and their youth pastors over the years? They wrote only a few lines on the first page, leaving a whole tablet of space empty. It was at once heartbreaking and eye-opening.

The biggest surprise of all came from a couple of students in particular. (We weren't surprised, however, that the two had similar reactions, since they were such good friends.) With a trembling grip on their tearstained papers, they approached us after youth group and asked if they could talk with us. They stood before us and wept.

Their confession sounded something like this: *"I had no idea how blessed I was! I've mocked my parents, made fun of them, and never really understood the gift they've given me to raise me in the faith. I DO remember what they've taught me! Even though I rolled my eyes when they'd repeat specific phrases of wisdom, their words went in! And I have them in me now! I know some things about God because of them! I need to apologize to my parents. And I need to start taking my freedom seriously. I need more of God's Word."*

Discernment is a vast topic—one far too involved to comprehensively address in just one chapter. But my prayer is that this chapter offers some food for thought. No matter what denominational lane you travel in, I think we can all agree on this: The only way we can *continually and consistently* discern God's heart and His voice is to *know Him, to walk intimately with Him, to immerse ourselves in His Word, and to be perpetually teachable before Him.*

➢

Discernment is not a matter of simply telling the difference between right and wrong; rather, it is telling the difference between right and almost right.

Charles Spurgeon

When someone claims to have the gift of discernment, how do you know they're not just speaking from their personal bias, personal experience, and cultural comforts? I've heard of Christians walking into a worship service that's more expressive than they're used to and quickly determining, *This is not of God.* Are you sure?

When we find ourselves in an uncomfortable setting, our instinctive reaction is to get back to our "known zone," the place where we know our way around, feel comfortable, and are somewhat in control. We may misinterpret a particular gathering as being *not of God* when in reality, it's just not our preference. Some like a more liturgical service, while others thrive in a more expressive one. Still others like a clean cut plan with no surprises. Isn't that okay? And is it okay for God to disrupt our tidy world on occasion? I sure hope so. Oswald Chambers writes:

> Never make a principle out of your experience; let God be as original with other people as He is with you.[2]

Many tribes and tongues love Jesus and celebrate Him in ways that are unique to their culture. May God give us biblical discernment to distinguish between personal discomfort and something that's actually in opposition to how God is moving at the moment. The tricky thing is, you may find yourself in a meeting where all kinds of people are genuinely encountering God in life-changing ways. At that same meeting, however, some might be operating in the flesh, distracting honest seekers (and it is those people who most often stand out to us).

It grieves my heart when Christians pridefully determine what's of God and what's not, based on cultural norms, wounded biases, personal comfort, or past experiences. Don't you think that Jesus perpetually surprised His disciples? He continually taught them to think outside the box of their cultural perceptions.

Consider the woman who broke the alabaster jar and anointed Jesus with tears and perfume. That was *way* out of context for the cultural norms of the day. As a result, people looked down their noses at her. But Jesus praised her. This dear, devoted woman prophetically prepared Jesus for burial. The religious leaders who had studied the Torah and knew it well wholly missed the move of God right in front of them.

King David danced wildly before the Lord—*way* out of context. Yet the Father loved David's passionate display of gratitude. Some celebrated with him while others held him in contempt. And so it goes today.

> Many times, Christians base their moral judgments on opinion, personal dislikes, or cultural bias rather than on the Word of God. When they do this, they show that their own faith is weak; they do not think that God is powerful enough to guide His own children. When we stand before God and give a personal account of our life, we won't be worried about what our Christian neighbor has done.[3]

If we find ourselves judging someone who is lavishly expressing themselves to God, we should tread carefully. We may face Jesus more as a foe than a friend at that moment because He inhabits the praises of His people.

So how do we discern whether something is out of order or just out of our comfort zone? We make it a daily practice to humble ourselves before God and ask Him to show us our blind spots, our biases, and any other core beliefs that keep us from discerning the beautiful, creative ways He's showing up in the world. And again, we immerse ourselves in the Word of God. The Word is our foundation.

If I could offer a caveat, though, it's this. You can know the Word and still miss the Person of Jesus Christ. Knowing the Word apart from the Person petrifies the heart. Knowing the Person of the Word purifies the heart.

You can know the Word and still **miss** the Person of Jesus Christ. **Knowing** the Word apart from the Person **petrifies** the heart. Knowing the Person of the Word **purifies** the heart.

In the beginning the Word already existed.
    The Word was with God,
    and the Word was God.
He existed in the beginning with God.
God created everything through him,
    and nothing was created except through him.
The Word gave life to everything that was created,
    and his life brought light to everyone.
The light shines in the darkness,
    and the darkness can never extinguish it.

John 1:1–5

Often (too often, in my opinion), in the name of discernment, I've heard the phrase *false teacher* thrown around in Christian circles. Why? Well, sometimes because it's true. Some preach a "gospel" message that's no gospel at all. And such a rebuke is warranted. But other times, the *false teacher* charge is leveled at someone simply because they theologically land in a different place around secondary issues.

When Jesus spoke of false teachers, He described them as wolves in sheep's clothing, people planted within the body of Christ with the intent to purposely deceive and lead people away from God.[4] They've filled their hearts with hatred and deceit. That's a far cry from a fellow believer who is wrestling through passages just as you are, trying to understand them. Isn't it possible to have theological differences with a brother or sister on nonessential issues without writing them off as a false teacher?

Doctrine is, of course, fundamental. But so is love. Consider the church at Ephesus in the book of Revelation. They guarded their doctrine but lost their love. For this the Spirit charged them to repent and to *look at how far they'd fallen.*[5]

I think a brother in Christ can be wrong about a particular doctrine while remaining a brother. Isn't our response to potential error a test of our own heart? If we instinctively default to pride, judgment, and believing the worst, we need to discern our own hearts. They may be wrong, but so are we, just in a different way. Scripture calls us to believe the best, not the worst; to make allowances; to be slow to speak and quick to listen; to not be quick to assess and assign; and to treasure mercy over judgment.[6]

If we see cause for concern in another, shouldn't we earnestly intercede for them since we *all* see as in a glass dimly?[7] Wouldn't that help the whole body of Christ grow up into all unity and maturity?

We all are wrong about some things. We're too quick to write each other off, thinking ourselves discerning. And the enemy loves it. Satan knows how powerful we are when we stand united as one. He relishes the pettiness and pride that divide us. Unity isn't conformity; it's unity on Christianity's cores. Unity is the bond of peace.[8] I humbly submit to you that a narrow mind isn't the same as the narrow path.

In essentials unity. In non-essentials, liberty. In all things, charity.[9]

⤳

When you hear that someone has the gift of discernment, you might wonder whether you have it as well. The *gift* of discernment spoken of in Scripture refers specifically to the supernatural ability to distinguish between the Spirit's influence and the enemy's demonic influence. Here's the passage referenced:

There are different kinds of spiritual gifts, but the same Spirit is the source of them all. There are different kinds of service, but we serve the same Lord. God works in different ways, but it is the same God who does the work in all of us.

A spiritual gift is given to each of us so we can help each other. To one person the Spirit gives the ability to give wise advice; to another the same Spirit gives a message of special knowledge. The same Spirit gives great faith to another, and to someone else the one Spirit gives the gift of healing. He gives one person the power to perform miracles, and another the ability to prophesy. He gives someone else the ability to discern whether a message is from the Spirit of God or from another spirit. Still another person is given the ability to speak in unknown languages, while another is given the ability to interpret what is being said. It is the one and only Spirit who distributes all these gifts. He alone decides which gift each person should have.

1 Corinthians 12:4–11

The word *discern* in the passage above is translated from the Greek *diakrisis*, which means distinguishing, discerning, differentiation, passing judgment.[10]

God imparted this gift when He poured out His Spirit on the church. This gift is highly needed in the body of Christ, given our tendency toward excess and our bent to walk in the flesh. Where the Spirit of the Lord is, there is freedom (2 Corinthians 3:17).

Amazing things happen when the Holy Spirit moves in our midst! Unfortunately, when people—under the guise of Christianity—operate in the flesh, there is disorder. Giving the enemy access to mimic spiritual gifts, introduce false doctrines, and confuse the saints is destructive.

> Let those who are wise understand these things.
> Let those with discernment listen carefully.
> The paths of the LORD are true and right,
> and righteous people live by walking in them.
> But in those paths sinners stumble and fall.

Hosea 14:9

➤

The Bible calls all of us—every believer—to live a life of discernment. According to Scripture, there are varying aspects of godly perception that we need to navigate life behind enemy lines.

For example, in the book of Philippians, Paul prayed that our love would abound more and more that we may continue growing in both knowledge and discernment.[11] The Greek word for *discernment* in this verse, *aísthēsis*, is different from the one used in the "gifts" passage. This word *aísthēsis* connects our capacity for the love of God with a heightened perception of the things of the Spirit. It also speaks of accumulated wisdom, knowledge, and insights acquired from growing in the things of God. This kind of discernment connects to both our senses and our intellect. Isn't that just beautiful? The more you grow in love, the more you grow in divine insight.

God charges us to discern our own hearts when we come to the communion table[12] and to renew our minds so that we can discern right from wrong, good from evil.[13] The Greek word for discernment in these two verses is the same word used in the "gifts" passage.

In other words, we need to discern the fleshly departures in ourselves as clearly as we try to determine them in others. In fact, if someone claims to be in-the-know about everyone else but rarely looks at themself, they are not as discerning as they may imagine.

And if we believe that only a select few Christ-followers possess the *gift* of discernment, we might relax our conviction and even miss the divine invitation to grow with God in this vital virtue. Maturity involves a growing capacity not only to discern evil counterfeits but also to perceive genuine movements of God. Even when they're outside our comfort zone.

> When the Spirit of truth comes, he will guide you into all truth. He will not speak on his own but will tell you what he has heard. He will tell you about the future.
>
> John 16:13

Prayerful Reflective Questions

1. *Lord, sometimes I second-guess what You're showing me because I give more weight to the thoughts of those around me than I do to Your Spirit within me. Have I done that lately, Lord? Speak to me.*

2. *Jesus, will You show me where I've misjudged a situation based on my personal biases?*

3. *Lord, have I made an idol out of my comfort zone and missed an opportunity to see You at work?*

4. *Father, whom have I judged that You've called me to pray for?*

The Humble Way: Consider, in the Gospels, how often people feared change when Jesus came to town. For instance, Jesus healed a demoniac who was a danger to himself and the townspeople, and how did the people respond? They begged Him to leave. We have our own fears around the seemingly unpredictable nature of God. He changes not, yet He's anything *but* predictable. And it's our love of comfort and control that so often keeps us from knowing Him in a way that radically changes us.

> You must also be willing to take your ideas of what the journey will be like and tear them into tiny pieces, for nothing on the itinerary will happen as you expect.
> Your Guide will not keep to any beaten path. He will lead you through ways you would never have dreamed your eyes would see. He knows no fear, and He expects you to fear nothing while He is with you.[14]

Jesus flipped tables. Confronted religious leaders. Talked to a lame man about his sin. Rebuked one of His closest friends and said, "Get behind Me, Satan!" He raised the dead. Healed the sick. And multiplied loaves and fishes. He ate and drank with sinners, knowing what that would do to His reputation.

Consider the various ways Jesus showed up in people's lives, and discern which one of these would be most uncomfortable to you.

106

Write out a prayer, inviting God to do that very thing in your life. Any time Jesus moves in your midst, you're better for it. Trust His love. Follow His lead.

Discern the Fiery Arrows: Pause here and ask God to show you how, in the name of discernment, the body of Christ has wounded its own. Identify, as best you can, the enemy's intent behind these arrows. Write out a prayer for the body of Christ. Before you write out your prayer, read Jesus' heartfelt prayer for you and me.

> Make them holy by your truth; teach them your word, which is truth. Just as you sent me into the world, I am sending them into the world. And I give myself as a holy sacrifice for them so they can be made holy by your truth.
>
> I am praying not only for these disciples but also for all who will ever believe in me through their message. I pray that they will all be one, just as you and I are one—as you are in me, Father, and I am in you. And may they be in us so that the world will believe you sent me.
>
> John 17:17–21

Say NO! Consider the collateral damage in the body of Christ over the issue of discernment. Contrary to the cultural phrases "your truth" and "my truth," there's really only *the* Truth, and it's Jesus. Pause here and ask the Lord to search your heart. Repent of any prideful or judgmental attitudes that have embedded in your soul. You may not see them right now, but if you sincerely want a pure heart, God will lovingly speak to you.

As someone who travels across denominational lines, I will say that those in the conservative reformed camp often judge charismatics for being loony and addicted to sensationalism (and that's sometimes true, but not always). And charismatics sometimes judge those in the reformed/cessation camp as being Bible snobs and Christian bullies (and that's sometimes true, but not always).

We'll never grow beyond the ungodly biases that we refuse to acknowledge. Also, it's quite possible to discern something in the spirit (to be quite right about what you see), and then to react in the flesh (to be quite wrong about what you do with the information God has imparted to you). Dare to get real and honest before the Lord. Then pick up your shield and intercede for Christ's precious body of believers. For the sake of the kingdom, say no to the enemy. Say yes to God. Write out your prayer.

Say **YES!** There's so much power in the YES that we give to God. Consider these beautiful examples of godly discernment from Scripture:

- Abraham discerned that in order to lay hold of the promises of God, he needed to surrender control in every area of his life and follow God into the unknown. (See Genesis 12.)
- Abraham discerned that God's promise was absolutely true, so he dared to surrender his dream (his son) to God, trusting He'd fulfill every word of His promise. (See Genesis 22:1 24.)
- Joseph discerned that what his brothers meant for evil, God turned for good. (See Genesis 50:20.)
- Ruth discerned that God was the One True God and left everything she knew to follow a God she could not see. (See Ruth 1:16.)
- David discerned that Goliath's intimidation had both national and spiritual consequences and trusted God to deliver him. (See 1 Samuel 17.)
- David discerned that even though Saul was trying to kill him, and God had promised David the role of king, it wasn't his for the taking; it was God's for the giving. He trusted God's timing. (See 1 Samuel 24.)

- Elijah discerned—in the face of intense threat—that when you're on the Lord's side, the odds against you are meaningless. He prayed that God would open the eyes of his servant so he also could believe. (See 2 Kings 6:16.)
- Anna and Simeon discerned that the Messiah had come when He was only a baby (and hadn't done a thing yet), while the religious leaders saw His miracles and missed Him completely. (See Luke 2:22–38.)
- Paul discerned that the gospel was also for Gentiles—a radical proposition back then. (See Acts 13.)
- Paul rebuked a fortune-teller for saying the right thing but in the wrong spirit. (See Acts 16:16–18.) Dr. Wiersbe writes, "Satan may speak the truth one minute and the next minute tell a lie, and the unsaved would not know the difference."[15]
- Paul discerned that God called him to testify in Rome and therefore knew he'd survive the storm. (See Acts 27, 28.)

Your assignment here is twofold: First, spend some time with the Lord, and ask Him to show you a few instances when you really heard Him and acted upon His direction. Do you know how precious your faith and your obedience are to Him? I submit that the more you cultivate a listening life, the more you'll hear what He has to say (and the more frequently He'll use you).

Second, pray through this verse and then write out a paraphrased declaration that fills your heart with faith. I've provided an example.

> The Lord God has given Me
> The tongue of the learned,
> That I should know how to speak
> A word in season to him who is weary.
> He awakens Me morning by morning,
> He awakens My ear
> To hear as the learned.
> The Lord God has opened My ear;

And I was not rebellious,
Nor did I turn away.

Isaiah 50:4–5 NKJV

Paraphrased Declaration:

Because I am filled with the Spirit of the Living God, I continually walk in His way! I'm sensitive to His Spirit. I know the word that sustains the weary. I speak and captives are set free! Each and every morning I meet with my God and He speaks to me. My heart is receptive. I will not refuse God's correction and direction. I'm ever and always listening to the Spirit of God within me.

Personalized Prayer

Father God, have I made an idol of control, respectability, or saving face? Have I prided myself in discernment when in reality, I've only judged that which I've not tried to understand? What does it look like to walk in biblical unity with brothers and sisters who land in a different place than I do on the nonessentials? Lord, how can I honor Your desire for oneness on a deeper level? Awaken my heart. Heighten my discernment. Help me to build some bridges. And please grow Your discernment in me that I may add strength to the church and stand in the gap against error. In Your precious name, I pray. Amen.

Spiritual Intelligence Training
SERVE AN AUDIENCE OF ONE

1. Read Daniel 6:1–5 and consider how often it happens that right before a promotion, enemy opposition comes. Why was Daniel in a position to be promoted? Revisit that for a moment.

2. In 1 Corinthians 16:9, Paul put it this way: "There is a wide-open door for a great work here, although many oppose me."

    a. What kinds of opportunities has God put before you in recent days?

    b. What kind of opposition are you facing?

3. Read Daniel 6:4–5 and prayerfully consider this reality. The deeper you go into the things of God and the more committed you are to His ways, the bigger the target you will become for the enemy of your soul. But have no fear. What an honor to live a life so above reproach that others have a hard time finding fault with you! Do you think Daniel knew these men were jealous of him and were scheming behind his back? Write down your thoughts.

4. Read Isaiah 54:17 and recommit your life and your reputation to the God who sees and vindicates His children. Do you trust that God will have your back? Write down your thoughts.

5. Read Daniel 6:6–11 and consider Daniel's response (he knelt, he prayed, and he gave thanks to God, *the way he'd always done*). If you were suddenly under fire from someone who opposed you, what things would you continue to do that you're doing today?

6. Read Daniel 6:12–18 and notice the king's response to Daniel's plight. Even though the king had been duped into this terrible decree, he no doubt knew which of his servants had moral clarity and which ones didn't (surely even more so after this situation). We live in a day when manipulation and corruption run amok, and truth is thrown to the ground (see Daniel 8:12). The Bible predicts that a great deception will occur in the latter days, and we see it today.

Pause here and ask God if you've gotten caught up in any form of groupthink that doesn't reflect His Word and His heart. Write down your thoughts.

7. Read Daniel 6:19–28 and notice how Daniel honored the king who, because of his ego and naïveté, had ordered Daniel thrown into the pit. Daniel, above all, glorified God. An earthly king witnessed the power of the ultimate King because one man was determined to honor his King. This is not to say that we agree with or endorse everything our leaders do, but rather, that we come to truly care about their souls and seek to honor God in the way we live out our lives under their rule. Too often, Christians absolve themselves from God's call to honor and respect because they so fiercely disagree with their leaders' policies. It always goes back to the fruit. Does our behavior and do our words reflect the fruit of the Spirit? If we're sincere Christ-followers, the fruit will be evident. The more anchored we are to the goodness of God, the more fiercely we'll trust the faithfulness of God. Write out King Darius's decree in a personalized way (vv. 25–27).

SIX

Navigating the Long Battle

Stay the Course

One of two things happens over time. Either your theology will conform to your reality, and your expectations will get smaller and smaller until you can hardly believe God for anything. Or your reality will conform to your theology, and your expectations will get bigger and bigger until you can believe God for absolutely everything![1]

Most mornings I wake up and know within a minute or two what kind of day it will be for me symptom-wise. I look forward to the day when I wake up and it doesn't even occur to me to wonder such things. Even so, I'm learning to find Jesus on the battlefield. I'm learning to embrace joy in the not-yet. And, in hindsight, I am beginning to see some of the benefits of the battle. Here's an excerpt from one of my journals:

The long battle makes whiners of some and warriors of others. I could easily be the whiner, but I'm determined to be a warrior. When longing and lament give way to grumbling and comparing, we quickly lose strength and precious ground. When literal soldiers fight in a literal war, they're in the trenches together. They build a camaraderie that makes them stronger together. They win and they lose together. Unfortunately, for those of us in spiritual battles, it's quite different. We find ourselves side by side with folks who seem to be living it up, with no apparent cares or concerns. We mingle with those who seem to easily possess what we've lacked for so long. It's hard to admit, and maybe this is my own pain filter, but sometimes you get the sense that while some feel a little bad for you, they kind of assume you deserve your lot; you must have missed a step. Still, you walk alongside others who barely notice that you're bleeding under your armor. The long battle can be lonely at times. I notice for me that when my longing and lament lead me to a place of despair, I need to step back and remember God's glorious, extraordinary greatness, His majesty and kindness, and His faithfulness to His promises. God is writing me into the unfathomable, historic kingdom story that He's crafting for all time. My place in His heart and in this story matters greatly. Therefore, how I steward this long battle matters significantly in the eternal story God is writing for His people. The things I long for now, I'll one day enjoy in heaven. Getting my way on earth isn't God's ultimate goal for me. Expanding His kingdom is. I've got work to do. Promises to believe. Faith to engage. Love to give. And intimacy to enjoy. Dear Father, I delight in You. I trust You with the longings of my heart. I refuse to count the days of my journey (it only weakens me and brings me despair). I'll count my blessings instead. Without a doubt—because I belong to You—I know that my future days will be far more glorious than my former days. And my former days are behind me. I'm still standing. I still believe. And I look forward with holy expectancy. Even now, You're answering the prayers of Your children around the world and bringing forth a glorious plan that one day will leave us all breathless. So as the Scriptures say, I will be joyful in hope, patient in affliction, and constant in prayer (Romans 12:12). I must trust You. And so, I trust You with my whole heart. In Your Son's matchless name, I pray. Amen.

But blessed are those who trust in the LORD
    and have made the LORD their hope and confidence.
They are like trees planted along a riverbank,
    with roots that reach deep into the water.
Such trees are not bothered by the heat
    or worried by long months of drought.
Their leaves stay green,
    and they never stop producing fruit.

Jeremiah 17:7–8

Keep Your Heart in It

In 1 Samuel, we read about precious Hannah, who couldn't have children. Imagine the heartbreak for this dear girl. Today, when someone battles infertility, their plight ignites all kinds of compassion and care. In biblical times, barrenness equaled cursedness (not blessedness). To have an empty womb and a broken heart seems burden enough. But to have other women judge, gossip, and wrongly assess your situation seems unbearable. Add to Hannah's distress her husband's other wife, who practically got pregnant just by thinking about it. (Not really, but it sure seemed that way.)

Scripture tells us that this woman not only bore plenty of children, but she also flaunted her blessing in Hannah's face until Hannah broke down and sobbed. Nothing worse than a petty, vindictive woman. Year after year, Hannah endured emotional torment and profound heartbreak. Where was God in this?

He was setting the stage for a significant breakthrough.

Let's pick up the story here and see what we can learn about ourselves and about God when we're in the long battle:

Once after a sacrificial meal at Shiloh, Hannah got up and went to pray. Eli the priest was sitting at his customary place beside the entrance of the Tabernacle. Hannah was in deep anguish, crying bitterly as she prayed to the LORD.

1 Samuel 1:9–10

Hannah turned to the Lord. She didn't numb out, check out, or fall out of the race. She ran to the Lord and poured out her heart to Him. We run a great risk of losing precious traction when we turn to the left or the right and indulge in that which weakens us. It's easy and tempting to do. Why not treat ourselves to a few indulgences here and there for all the hardship we've endured? Nothing wrong with a few treats now and then. But I think we all know the difference between freedom within self-control and indulging because-I-deserve-more-than-God-is-giving-me-at-the-moment, or so-I-don't-have-to-face-what-I'm-feeling-beneath-the-surface. The painful reality is this: Indulgence—wrongly motivated consumption that feeds the flesh—always weakens the spirit, which causes us to drift unaware.

Let's look at the response of Eli, the high priest, to Hannah:

As she was praying to the LORD, Eli watched her. Seeing her lips moving but hearing no sound, he thought she had been drinking. "Must you come here drunk?" he demanded. "Throw away your wine!"

1 Samuel 1:12–14

Scoot a little closer and look at that verse one more time. Eli *saw* but didn't *hear*, so he *thought* wrongly about the situation. When we see without hearing, our assessments will always lack clarity. I'm sure you've felt the sting of someone who thinks they have a good read on your suffering. They *see* what you're going through, but they don't *hear* you. So they draw wrong conclusions about your trials (think Job's friends).

Eli's accusation both intrigues me and breaks my heart. Eli's own sons were drinking in the temple, defiling the sacrifices with no fear of God. This, I'm sure, greatly grieved Eli, who viewed dear Hannah

Indulgence—**wrongly** motivated consumption that **feeds** the flesh—always **weakens** the spirit, which causes us to drift **unaware**.

through his own pain filter. Because his sons were often drunk, he *assumed* Hannah was too.

We must deal with the pain filters that find their way into our perspective when the journey is long and arduous. If we don't, we'll not only wrongly assess our own suffering, but we'll also make wrong assumptions about others, which adds to their burden. We must learn how to steward our pain in a way that brings about healing, redemption, and holy expectancy. This glorifies God and infuriates the enemy. And the truth is, our skewed perspectives almost always trace back to heartache and disappointment with God. He could have; why didn't He? He can; why doesn't He? Where is He?

In my book *Your Powerful Prayers: Reaching the Heart of God with Bold and Humble Faith*, I write about a time when I was literally on the floor, facedown on the carpet, asking those very questions. Then suddenly, a whisper fluttered across my heart. *Susie, you can ask Me any question any time, day or night. But these questions are killing you. I want you to ask Me better questions.* Better questions? Where might I find those? He whispered once again: *Try these:*

- *What is this disappointment saying to me that's not true?*
- *What is this disappointment saying about me that's not true?*
- *What is this disappointment saying to me about God that's not true?*

Do some work around these questions and remember while you're at it that you're processing your pain with a God who is filled with compassion, abounding in love, rich with wisdom, and full of grace. He welcomes the wrestle, and He'll bring truth to your soul.

➤

We're continually presented opportunities to either accuse God or trust Him. It's especially tempting to wrongly frame your life and

We're **continually** presented opportunities to either **accuse** God or **trust** Him.

your trials when you're weary and tired of it all. That's when your mind goes to *how long and how little* (how long you've been on this journey and how little ground you've gained).

When we're tired of the long fight, we instinctively begin to add up the days, the years, and the seasons of our trial. Where does that lead us? Right into the ditch of despair. When you look up and see a discrepancy between how others live and how you struggle, between what they're enjoying and what you're enduring, it can take the wind right out of your sails.

The thing is, though these perspectives feel true, they're only partially true. Yes, some people are enjoying the best season of their lives while you army crawl through yours (but for all of us, seasons change). Yes, God allows us to go for long periods without seeing the sun. Yes, He allows us to endure hardships that feel like they might swallow us whole. And yes, He often seems to show up when we're well past our breaking point.

But the *truest* thing is this: God is sovereignly in control. He will have His way and have the final say. This same unrivaled, remarkable, powerful God loves you with a love so fierce that no demon in hell will ultimately prevail against you. You are an overcomer.

You may get knocked down, but God will give you the grace to get back up again. You may lose a battle, but Jesus has already won the war. You may mess up, but Jesus' blood cleans you up. You may repeatedly lose heart, but God is the strength of your heart and your portion forever.[2] You are a part of the conquering kingdom!

Your trials are achieving something in you that you cannot even fathom, and if you could, you'd be fiercely determined to hold on to faith, to trust Jesus with your life, and to tell that enemy what's what. If you could see the end from the beginning, your confidence and courage would soar.

You, dear one, *will see God's majesty*—His meticulous attention to detail—on that Great Day. Your battles combined with your faith create an explosion in the heavenly realm. When God pulls back the sky and reveals His glory to the world, you will be standing with Him! The world will gasp, and so will you. Imagine it!

> Yet what we suffer now is nothing compared to the glory he will reveal to us later. For all creation is waiting eagerly for that future day when God will reveal who his children really are.
>
> Romans 8:18–19

The word *reveal* is used twice in this verse. Our suffering is somehow connected to the grand revealing of God's glory. The word *reveal* means *to uncover, to make known, to make manifest.* God will show the world a glory it has not yet seen, and every knee will bow, and every tongue will confess that Jesus is the Lord of all. The second time the word *reveal* is used (same Greek word) speaks of the great revealing of God's people. Same thing: to uncover, to make known. To make manifest in the most glorious way. Our God has so grafted us into His family that He plans to *reveal* His glory and His children on the same day.

> Consider the kind of extravagant love the Father has lavished on us—He calls us children of God! It's true; we are His *beloved* children. And in the same way the world didn't recognize Him, the world does not recognize us either. My loved ones, *we have been adopted into God's family; and* we are officially His children now. The full picture of our destiny is not yet clear, but we know this much: when Jesus appears, we will be like Him because we will see Him just as He is. All those who focus their hopes on Him *and His coming* seek to purify themselves just as He is pure.
>
> 1 John 3:1–3 VOICE

Yes, we encounter trials as we navigate life in a fallen world, but every aspect of our stories is about to be redeemed. As my friend John Eldredge said on my show a while back, one day, "your story will be told rightly."[3] Goodness is coming, friend. Believe it. Amen!

Our enemy knows this and hates it. He'll stop at nothing to derail our perspective in hopes of diminishing our influence. Satan figures that if he can't steal our eternity, he can at least destroy our influence in hopes of stealing some of our eternal rewards. Our story is never just about us. When the enemy steals from us, he also steals from others because our lives are so intertwined with our fellow believers. That's why he'll stop at nothing to achieve his purposes. He finds us when we're hungry, angry, lonely, and tired, and he sows the life-draining seeds of discouragement, despair, and unbelief along with bitterness, pride, and unforgiveness. When we act on those feelings, we give our enemy easy access to steal us dry, which costs others as well. This is why it's so essential to think eternity, hold fast to our identity, and stand in our authority (more on that in the next chapter).

Thankfully, God wastes nothing, misses nothing, overlooks nothing. He's working even now—training us for battle, redeeming our hardships, and changing us from glory to glory—and He loves our faith. When we are in Christ, Christ is in us! We have the Spirit of the Living God mightily at work in us![4] As we walk intimately with Him and respond to His supernatural guidance and correction in our lives, our vision increasingly clarifies, our hearts more deeply understand, and our faith continually arises. We get wiser to the enemy's schemes and get stronger in battle.

> But whenever someone turns to the Lord, the veil is taken away. For the Lord is the Spirit, and wherever the Spirit of the Lord is, there is freedom. So all of us who have had that veil removed can see and reflect the glory of the Lord. And the Lord—who is the Spirit—makes us more and more like him as we are changed into his glorious image.
>
> 2 Corinthians 3:16–18

We started this chapter by looking at Hannah, who had an empty womb and a broken heart. But then she received a word from the

Lord. She would have a son. What she didn't know was that her son Samuel—whom she dedicated to the Lord—would become one of the greatest prophets of all time. Hannah had no idea how divine and deliberate God's delays in her life were. You and I cannot fathom how significant and purposeful our not-yets are to the greater kingdom narrative, of which God is the Author! Our story is never just about us. And the sooner we trust God more than we do our puny perspective, the sooner we will move into that place of faith where His promises become sturdier than our circumstances. Read this powerful insight from Dr. Jack Hayford:

> God uses the burden of Hannah's heart to bring a surprisingly larger solution to the burden of His own heart. Barrenness was not only Hannah's condition, but Israel's condition as well. It was a season of spiritual need with little prophetic activity . . . and God sought a voice to speak on His behalf to His people. *Hannah could not know that her intense intercession for a child was moving in concert with God*—bringing her a son, but also bringing forth the will and blessing of God for a whole nation. As she entrusts the longings of her heart to God, He moves on <u>her</u> behalf, but also advances His larger plan through her at the same time.[5]

You cannot fully know—this side of heaven—how important your faith is to the greater kingdom story, but believe it anyway. God is up to something magnificent.

Prayerful Reflective Questions

1. *Precious Father, please show me the dim places in my perspective. From whom do I need to learn? What do I need to hear? What do You long for me to see?*
2. *How has this long battle taken a toll on my soul? What in me needs Your healing touch?*

3. *Father, how do the burdens of my heart reflect the greater burden of Your heart?*

4. *Lord, will You give me glimpses of Your divinely powerful story in the coming days? Open my eyes to see what You're up to in our day!*

The Humble Way: It's profoundly essential—especially in the long battle—to keep yourself in the love of Christ. Of course, Scripture says that nothing can ever separate us from His love, but I'm referring to our own heart condition before the Lord. Scripture also says, "Hope deferred makes the heart sick, but a dream fulfilled is a tree of life" (Proverbs 13:12). It's hard to wait a long time for your breakthrough. Especially when you see the culture imploding all around you. If we're not careful, seeds of despair will take root. We may find ourselves deeply hurt by God because He hasn't rescued us yet. We can't make this journey alone. We need others. And they need us. Read this passage from Jude, vv. 20–21:

> But you, dear friends, must build each other up in your most holy faith, pray in the power of the Holy Spirit, and await the mercy of our Lord Jesus Christ, who will bring you eternal life. In this way, you will keep yourselves safe in God's love.

Here's your assignment: First, spend some extended time with the Lord and ask Him to show you your heart. Do you feel cared for by God? Safe in His love? Noticed by Him? Because you are. So if your feelings toward God contradict what's true about Him, just be honest about that and let Him lead you to a place of peace and assurance. Second, reach out to two people. Make one a person who needs what you have to offer. Build her up in the most holy faith, and pray in the power of the Holy Spirit. Then reach out to someone who has the kind of faith you need right now and be honest about where you're at and what you need. Pray together.

Write out your prayer below and ask God to help you identify the two people on His heart for you.

Discern the Fiery Arrows: Sometimes we need to minimize our inputs to better discern the enemy's intent and target (e.g., intent: to discourage you; target: your kids). For example, when we're overexposed to social media, negative news, and acidic or divisive people, we tend to have one of two responses. One, we get pulled in so deep that we find ourselves in an echo chamber of sorts. We react to those on the other side. We dig in our heels with our opinions. We pride ourselves on our rightness. And before we know it, we no longer feel love or compassion or concern for the soul we oppose. The enemy's intent? To lead us away from love and into fear, away from compassionate concern, and into comparison. It's hard to hear from the Lord or be effective in battle when we're in such a place.

A second response to too much of the wrong input is just plain despair. You see the state of the world, or you notice how blessed everybody else seems to be, and you're left without a sense of hope, faith, or expectancy. As believers, we are called by God to discern truth from lie, fact from fiction, photoshopped-façade from authentic, humble, real life.

Fasting from the news and social media allows you to clear the air, quiet your heart, and listen to Jesus more intently. Right now, the Holy Spirit is interceding for you with groanings too deep for words.[6] What do you suppose He's saying? What's He praying? Pause here and prayerfully consider the passage below. As you do, ask God to show you His heart for you, the enemy's strategy against you, and what God wants you to do about it.

> Likewise the Spirit also helps in our weaknesses. For we do not know what we should pray for as we ought, but the Spirit Himself makes intercession for us with groanings which cannot be uttered. Now He who searches the hearts knows what the mind of the Spirit is, because He makes intercession for the saints according to the will of God.
>
> Romans 8:26–27 NKJV

Journal your thoughts and prayers here.

Say NO! God is the One who determines your battle strategy. You receive your marching orders from Him. There will be times when everyone else is running, and He'll charge you to rest. There will be times when your emotions compel you to run to the battle line, and your Father tells you to tuck yourself under His wing so He can fight for you. There will be other times when everything in you wants to hide, and He'll charge you to stand and fight. Since that's true, you can know that the enemy will always try to bait you to do the opposite of what God knows is best for you.

We'll be tempted toward self-pity, discouragement, entitlement, disillusionment, jealousy, and even laziness. The sooner the enemy can move us into such mindsets, the sooner he can snatch the treasures God has appointed for us in these valleys. Our enemy isn't just interested in defeating us. He intends to steal that which God has promised us. Pause here and ponder the verse below.

> We can rejoice, too, when we run into problems and trials, for we know that they help us develop endurance. And endurance develops strength of character, and character strengthens our confident hope of salvation. And this hope will not lead to disappointment. For we know how dearly God loves us, because he has given us the Holy Spirit to fill our hearts with his love.
>
> Romans 5:3–5

Your shield of faith is a powerful, supernatural weapon (see Ephesians 6:16). Raise it up and say no to the enemy of your soul! Prayerfully consider this: What do you need to say no to? Write out a faith declaration prayer.

Say YES! Our sword is our weapon of offense, and we know how to use it! Consider Dr. Jack Hayford's insights on Hannah's life once more. He explained how Hannah's burden reflected the greater burden of God's heart and how her prayers were actually moving in concert with God's prayers for the world. Amazingly, the answer to her prayers proved to be a significant answer to God's burden for His people. Ask God to help you see yourself in the bigger story.

People worldwide are struggling deeply in some of the same ways you've struggled. How might your intercession reflect God's heart and intentions for the world? Pause here and ponder the verse below. Notice how God's ability to do wondrous works is directly connected to the work we allow Him to do within us.

> Now all glory to God, who is able, through his mighty power at work within us, to accomplish infinitely more than we might ask or think. Glory to him in the church and in Christ Jesus through all generations forever and ever! Amen.
>
> Ephesians 3:20–21

How might God want to upgrade your level of intercession? Write out a prayer of faith on behalf of your brothers and sisters who are battling the way you are right now. Let faith arise and let your enemies be scattered!

Personalized Prayer

Precious Lord,

You're everything to me! Fill me afresh with the wonder of Your love. Show me how You're working in my day and in my life. Help me to rightly interpret my battles that I may last long and finish strong.

Remind me again and again that there's an end date to these trials. Lord, thank You for the blessings that are already mine because I've trusted You on this journey. You've made me stronger, wiser, and fiercer in my faith. You've taught me about Your promises and Your faithfulness and made me long for Your presence. Where would I be without You? Give me the courage and confidence to keep marching and believing and receiving all that You so lovingly pour out on Your children. In Your name, I pray. Amen.

Spiritual Intelligence Training
TRUST GOD'S TIMING

1. Over and over in Scripture, we see the painful delay between when God makes a promise and when He fulfills it. Those who wait on His timing receive the best of what God has for them. Those who rush ahead to grab a quick solution encounter more trouble than they bargained for. Let's start by looking up the following verses: Isaiah 43:1–3; Isaiah 64:4; Psalm 27:13–14; and Lamentations 3:25. What have you learned about God and about yourself during the waiting seasons?

2. In 1 Samuel, chapter 16, we read about when God told Samuel to anoint David as the next king. Read the whole chapter and answer the next two questions. Imagine how David must have felt to learn that his father didn't even bother to call him from the fields when the prophet first arrived. Yet even his father's skewed perspective wouldn't hinder God's ultimate plan. God is meticulously and attentively preparing you for His purposes, even if others don't notice. David was faithfully tending to his current assignment when God anointed him for what would be his next assignment. What is your current assignment? What's your sense about God's timing?

3. Imagine David's surprise when he was summoned to the palace to play music for the king. Was this God's way of bringing him into the palace? While God definitely used this assignment to prepare David for palace life, David would end up running for his life. Read 1 Samuel 20. Oftentimes, after God gives us a glimpse of His promise, He leads us in the opposite direction. Why do you suppose God allowed King Saul to misuse his power in a way that cost David so much? David was the man God wanted in leadership, yet He allowed David to suffer much hardship. Write down your thoughts.

4. Read 1 Samuel 24 and answer the following questions:

    a. *As it happened,* Saul entered the very cave where David and his men were hiding. Saul decided to relieve himself, putting himself in a vulnerable position. This is the man who'd unjustly and repeatedly tried to kill David, though David had done nothing wrong. David's men were convinced God had delivered Saul into his hands. What do you think?

    b. Sometimes when our dream is within our reach, we think nothing of grabbing for it without consulting God first. If He promised it and He delivered it, it's time to grab hold of it, right? Not always. How might things have played out if David had wrongly interpreted the signs and killed Saul?

    c. David feared God and trusted His timing no matter what. How did he develop such a conviction?

    d. How willing are you to actively, expectantly, and humbly *wait* for God to fulfill His promise to you?

5. It's interesting how, even though Saul admitted his wrongdoing and confessed that David was far more righteous than he, David stayed in the wilderness. In spite of that significant breakthrough, it still wasn't time for him to take the throne. How did this conflict prepare David to one day take the throne?

6. Read 2 Samuel 5:1–4 and consider this: God anointed David as a young man to be the next king, then for years David lived as an outlaw before God finally opened the door and made him king of Israel. There's always a cost and a time of preparation for serving God in greater ways. How has God prepared you for what you're doing now? How does it seem He's preparing you for future service?

7. In 2 Samuel 5:6–12 we read that when David approached the gates to the city of Jebus, the soldiers told him, "You will *never* get in here!" Even so, David conquered the city and renamed it the City of David, Jerusalem. This important city would become the birthplace of Christianity. Let's look at verse 12 together: "David realized that the

LORD had confirmed him as king over Israel and had blessed his king-dom **for the sake of his people Israel**" (emphasis mine).

    a. We must remember that locked gates mean nothing when God says it's time to walk through them. What obstacles are you facing today? What is God telling you to do?

    b. God trains us and prepares us for Promised Land living not just for us, but for the sake of those we're appointed to influence. Few are willing to pay the price to go all-in with God. Yet this world needs more kingdom influencers. Have you put any lim-its on your relationship with God? Write down your thoughts (and maybe a prayer too).

SEVEN

You Have an Enemy

Stay True

———

No matter how dark our night, God's morning always comes.
No matter how downcast we may feel, God's presence is always with us.
No matter how desperate our circumstances, God's power always
prevails.[1]

You're standing on the battlefield, in an arena. You look to the
left and right and see several arched doorways with their gates
open. Though you don't see them yet, you hear hungry lions roar-
ing in the shadows. You sense they're about to be unleashed into
the arena to attack you for sport. In the far distance, you see the
enemy himself coming toward you. He's smirking, confident, and
headed straight for you. Your breathing becomes shallow. Prick-
les crawl up your spine. You notice that over each of the arched
doorways are words: *Worry. Fear. Abandonment. What If?* And
others.

You're outnumbered and immediately feel overwhelmed.

But then you remember Jesus' words.

Look, I have given you authority over all the power of the enemy, and you can walk among snakes and scorpions and crush them. Nothing will injure you.

Luke 10:19

Suddenly, a holy surge of confidence shoots through you. You look over at the first doorway, where you hear the lion roar. You point to it, and with the authority God has given you, declare, "I say NO to worry! I close that door, in Jesus' name!" The gate thunders down and shakes the ground. The lion slinks back in the shadows and loses his roar. Then you look at the *Fear* doorway and do the same: "I say NO to fear! I close that door, in Jesus' name!" One by one, you use your authority to bring down each gate. And with every doorway that closes, the lions' roars fade. Something else happens too. You notice that as the enemy gets closer, he's also shrinking. He's losing steam.

When the enemy's weapons of fear, intimidation, and deception no longer work on us, he loses power over us.

Still, he keeps coming toward you, holding a notebook crammed with information about you. He's studied you your whole life. He knows what makes you weak, sad, frightened, and discouraged. And he's headed your way.

But suddenly, you feel a warmth on your face and turn your eyes toward the glow coming from your right. You look over to see a beautiful, glimmering gate, and the words from Scripture come to mind: *"Open up, ancient gates! Open up, ancient doors, and let the King of glory enter!"*[2] Faith rises up in you, and you shout, "Open up, ancient gates! And let the King of glory enter!" To your pure delight, in comes Jesus with eyes of fire, face aglow, and clothes as white as snow. His smile reaches up to His eyes. He's not stressed over this battle. He's thrilled to see you.

He steps in front of you and prepares a table for you in the presence of your enemy (see Psalm 23:5). He seats you at the table, a place of honor. He brings out the bread, the wine, and the fruit.

136

You look at the bread, and right away, you remember that He was broken that you might be made whole. You recall Jesus' words when He said, *"My nourishment comes from doing the will of God, who sent me."*[3] And you remember how He multiplied the loaves and the fishes. You find great significance in this sacred gift of bread on the battlefield.

Then you look at the chalice of wine. By His stripes, you are healed. Because of His shed blood and victory on the cross, you are saved. You will overcome by the blood of the Lamb and the word of your testimony, and you will learn to love Him more than you love your very life. Perfect love casts out fear.[4] The more you grow acquainted with God's love, the less you're derailed by your fears.

You look into your Savior's eyes and find yourself strengthened by the divine confidence that emanates from Him. You realize there's more power in one drop of the Savior's blood than in all of hell's evil combined. And His blood courses through your veins! You are alive in Christ. His resurrection power is active in you! Oh, to walk and even battle in the God-given power entrusted to you! You determine never to let fear win the day again.

The bountiful fruit reminds you of Jesus' words to His disciples and to you: *I've appointed you to bear fruit that lasts. It's to My Father's glory that you bear much fruit.* You were made for the abiding life. Fruit comes from intimacy with God. He wants to nourish the world through your beautiful life.

Bread. Wine. Fruit. Wholeness. Ministry. Multiplication. You are part of an otherworldly kingdom. It's no wonder the enemy works so hard to keep you living an earthbound life. If he can keep your gaze on the fears of this life, unloving people, and the stresses of your circumstances, you'll forget that there's so much more going on than meets the eye.

But when your spiritual eyes open, you realize that you've been given the power to actually do something about the circumstances in your midst. You're on to the enemy's schemes and his continual attempt to pull your gaze downward. You are part of the conquering

The more
you **grow**
acquainted with
God's **love**,
the less you're
derailed by your
fears.

army of the kingdom of heaven. You decide to look up and find your help and strength in Christ Jesus.

> I also pray that you will understand the incredible greatness of God's power for us who believe him. This is the same mighty power that raised Christ from the dead and seated him in the place of honor at God's right hand in the heavenly realms. Now he is far above any ruler or authority or power or leader or anything else—not only in this world but also in the world to come. God has put all things under the authority of Christ and has made him head over all things for the benefit of the church. And the church is his body; it is made full and complete by Christ, who fills all things everywhere with himself.
>
> Ephesians 1:19–23

Strongholds are broken. Captives are set free. The lost are found. You have work to do. You're recovering your roar. You refuse to be constantly kicked around by your enemy. You suddenly know and believe that this King you serve is far more powerful than you once thought. This means you now have the divine capacity to be mighty in battle.

Yes, the enemy can be a formidable foe. Yes, we sometimes have to engage in hand-to-hand combat when it feels as though our circumstances might crush us. But overwhelming victory belongs to us because we belong to Jesus, our King. Our Defender. Our Deliverer. Our Strong Tower.

> The name of the LORD is a fortified tower;
> the righteous run to it and are safe.
> Proverbs 18:10 NIV

Picture yourself running into the strong, fortified tower and the door disappearing behind you. There's no opening for the enemy to enter. Only God's children have access to this protected stronghold. You are safe in His care.

Spiritual warfare is not something to be taken lightly. The enemy destroys lives and even whole communities in places where evil is allowed to flourish. But one day, his schemes will be uncovered and wholly dismantled. He'll forever lose his power to deceive and destroy. Oh, I long for that day!

Yes. We have a very real enemy whose aim is to steal, kill, and destroy, as John 10:10 tells us.

But if we focus solely on *him* and how he's stirring up trouble, we'll lose heart and courage. We'll forget about the rest of that verse, where Jesus says, "But I've come that you might have life and live to the fullest" (my paraphrase). It's possible to abound in hope and joy and flourish in life even when we have an enemy hiding in the darkness, hoping to derail us.

That's not to say we won't endure seasons when it feels like the furies of hell are aimed at us. I'm in one such season right now. To be honest, it's been at once brutal and beautiful. I've absolutely hated parts of this battle and have at times wished God would just rescue me. But there's a big difference between relief for relief's sake and the supernatural redemption of our stories and hearts. I'm learning how to better use my sword and shield. I'm learning things about myself and about God that I'd somehow missed before.

When we find ourselves on the battlefield, we need to clear the field of the accompanying emotions and attitudes that make fighting and winning almost impossible. No one can do that for us. Fear has to leave. Worry too. Unforgiveness. Ungodly assumptions. Attitudes that usurp authority. Pride. Jealousy. Judgments. Idolatry. Hatred. Bitterness. And a host of other heart conditions that open the door to the enemy's influence in our lives. He is a legalist. If we give him the opportunity, he'll take it. Every time.

We also need to address our questions about God's goodness and faithfulness—ideally before the storms hit. But if not then, we'll surely need to reckon with these issues while we're under fire. God's

When we find ourselves on the **battlefield**, we need to **clear** the field of the accompanying emotions and attitudes that make **fighting** and **winning** almost impossible.

goodness and faithfulness are foundational to our victory in battle. Somehow, we need to settle it in our hearts that God is a profoundly good Father and that He will never forsake us.

We don't dictate our outcomes to Him. He decides what's best for us. But when we humble ourselves, when we hold fiercely to the truth of His Word, and when we engage our faith—whatever amount of faith we have at the moment—God moves. He responds. We find Him faithful. He breaks through exactly when the time is right and when our training is complete. And we'll see over and over again that His ways, His outcomes, His protection, and His provision are consistently motivated by His goodness and concern for us.

But we'll take plenty of unnecessary batterings if we move out of rank or forget what's true. To win in battle, we must diligently tend to the condition of our heart.

I love Eugene Peterson's paraphrase of this passage:

> Keep vigilant watch over your heart;
> > *that's* where life starts.
> Don't talk out of both sides of your mouth;
> > avoid careless banter, white lies, and gossip.
> Keep your eyes straight ahead;
> > ignore all sideshow distractions.
> Watch your step,
> > and the road will stretch out smooth before you.
> Look neither right nor left;
> > leave evil in the dust.
>
> Proverbs 4:23–27 MESSAGE

The Truth Sets Us Free and Keeps Us Free

Since the enemy cannot snatch away your eternal security, he'll do whatever he can to disrupt your peace in the present and rob you of your future eternal reward. If he can keep you stuck in the rut of reacting to your troubles in the flesh, he'll most certainly keep you from walking in the Spirit, which is where the true kingdom life happens.

The devil wants to hold you captive. He puts thoughts in your mind, hoping you'll rehearse them until they feel true. He goes after your identity, hoping you'll forget who you are so you'll make choices contrary to God's truth about you. He goes after God's goodness in seasons of hardship so you'll forget which way is up and lose sight of His promises. The enemy wants you to question: If God's not good, why would you expect Him to be so on your battlefield? To be unsure about this point will definitely destabilize you on the battlefield.

The devil frequently finds access in the hearts of others and uses them to distract and discourage the saints of God. He wants our gaze on the person and not on the enemy's schemes behind the scenes. We have one enemy, and it's the devil himself. As Scripture charges us to remember: Our battle is not against flesh and blood but against rulers and authorities and powers of this dark world (see Ephesians 6:12). Just as there's a hierarchy in the demonic world, there's one in the heavenly kingdom. When we learn to wage war, as Scripture teaches us, we become proficient in battle. Our capacity to win is tied directly to the renewal of our minds:

> We are human, but we don't wage war as humans do. We use God's mighty weapons, not worldly weapons, to knock down the strongholds of human reasoning and to destroy false arguments. We destroy every proud obstacle that keeps people from knowing God. We capture their rebellious thoughts and teach them to obey Christ.
>
> 2 Corinthians 10:3–5

Now more than ever, we need to be ruthless with mindsets and attitudes that are in direct conflict with God's heart, His Word, and His ways.

Behind every scheme is a lie. And behind every lie is an attempt to derail God's ultimate kingdom purposes on the earth. Our enemy will use any unsuspecting vessel he can find. What doors does he most often find open in the hearts of man? *Jealousy and selfish ambition.* These are the gateway sins that lead to all kinds of evil and manipulative behavior.

> For jealousy and selfishness are not God's kind of wisdom. Such things are earthly, unspiritual, and demonic. For wherever there is jealousy and selfish ambition, there you will find disorder and evil of every kind.
>
> James 3:15–16

If you find yourself on the receiving end of offense, accusation, or irritation because of someone's jealousy, the best thing you can do is to humble yourself before almighty God, knowing He'll be your best defense. Pray for that person until you have genuine compassion for them. They don't know what they're doing. Someday they will. Keep your heart pure and your mouth shut. Let God fight for you. In due time, the storm will pass, and you will walk in a new level of holy confidence.

Every time I've walked through such a season, I've pressed deeper into the truths of God's unconditional love, which always brings about more profound levels of healing and holiness. I've asked Him to cleanse and purify my heart—to remove from me the things that are accusable in me. I ask Him to lead me on the life-giving path He has for me. I often say that it takes a measure of humility to allow the fire to refine you when someone else is guilty of lighting the match. But why waste a perfectly good fire? And I've learned to pray earnestly for those who don't quite understand the damage they do when they choose judgment over mercy. God deals with people who, out of jealousy, stir up trouble. You stay the course.

If you take the bait of offense, if you blame others for your problems and feel justified in your hatred of specific people or groups, you've wandered onto enemy territory unarmed, just as your enemy hoped you would. Take one look on social media and you'll find that many, many Christians have taken this bait and have rendered themselves inoperable on the battlefield. In fact, some are doing much more harm than good because they're fighting in the flesh, accusing in the flesh, and justifying their attitudes, which are born of the flesh. Lord, have mercy.

The devil is a liar. That's his native tongue. And he's terrified of the truth. It's the life-giving, soul-altering, demon-destroying *truth* that the enemy is trying to steal from you. God's Word is a seed in our soil, and when we nurture it, guard it, water it, and weed the soil, that Word produces thirty, sixty, and sometimes one hundred times what was planted.[5] Imagine! When we treasure God's Word, we, in due time, find ourselves flourishing in the truth of His Word, regardless of what's going on in the world.

> But blessed are those who trust in the Lord
>   and have made the Lord their hope and confidence.
> They are like trees planted along a riverbank,
>   with roots that reach deep into the water.
> Such trees are not bothered by the heat
>   or worried by long months of drought.
> Their leaves stay green,
>   and they never stop producing fruit.
>   Jeremiah 17:7–8

Hell trembles at the thought of your being so deeply rooted and grounded in God that you learn to flourish in every season. The enemy quivers at the idea of you suddenly remembering that you're actually a mighty prayer warrior, fully equipped to dismantle the powers that oppose you and oppress others. The degree to which truth takes root in you will be the degree at which you start to win more than you lose. God's truth is the enemy's kryptonite.

The truth not only sets you free, but it also keeps you free.

We are in a day when right has become wrong, wrong has become right, and our shame has become our glory, just as Scripture states. We've got to keep our wits about us. We have to continually immerse ourselves in God's truth. We need to regularly say it, pray it, live it, and give it to others, so the enemy has no opportunity to snatch it from us. We need to cultivate the stewardship of listening to and learning from the Holy Spirit so that we increasingly grow in discernment and walk in the authority entrusted to us. The minute we're deceived is the moment the enemy makes his move. Read Jesus' sobering words out of Mark's gospel:

> Then he added, "Pay close attention to what you hear. The closer you listen, the more understanding you will be given—and you will receive even more. To those who listen to my teaching, more understanding will be given. But for those who are not listening, even what little understanding they have will be taken away from them."
>
> Mark 4:24–25

We can only listen to one voice at a time. When you're faithful to know God's voice and take to heart what He says, He will impart ever-increasing measures of revelation and understanding. What thoughts do you have on repeat these days? Whose voice rings loudest in your ear right now?

I'm convinced that the best way to win in battle is to enjoy deep intimacy with God so you're continually acquainted with His heart and His ways, and to grow proficient with your sword and shield. Scripture tells us that one of the reasons we have the Holy Spirit is to clearly discern the things God has freely given us.

> And we have received God's Spirit (not the world's spirit), so we can know the wonderful things God has freely given us.
>
> 1 Corinthians 2:12

Picture yourself growing in the knowledge of God, increasing in the wisdom of God, walking in greater measures of the power of God. The enemy shudders at the thought of it.

How do we defend land that we don't know is ours? What things has God freely given us? He promised us peace that passes understanding. Grace to abound in every good work. Healing and wholeness in our soul that cannot be explained except for the goodness of God. Power to mark our days. Love that changes our ways. And wisdom that doesn't come from this world. This, and so much more. These things are yours in Christ Jesus. Contend for them. Guard them. And get them back from the hands of the enemy if you've lost them.

At the beginning of this book, I mentioned that I originally wanted to organize the book around a faith declaration I wrote some time ago, but then I decided I needed a different approach. I have to say though, that given the battle I'm currently walking through, this faith declaration has been of great help to me. I've realized that when you go long enough under fire, you really do forget some of what's true about God and about you. So for those who may need a feisty faith reminder of who you are, this one is for you:

As a citizen of the heavenly kingdom,
An heir of God and joint-heir with Christ,
Filled with the Spirit of the Living God,
I speak with precision,
I pray with power,
I walk in authority.
I am anointed and appointed,
Blessed and beloved,
Bold and brave,
Called and courageous,
Because I know God is with me.
I will triumph over my enemy,
And I will stand with Jesus on that final day.

Prayerful Reflective Questions

1. *Lord, where have I trusted the enemy's threats more than I've trusted Your goodness in my life?*
2. *What attitudes or emotions have weakened me on the battlefield?*
3. *What promises are mine for the taking in this particular season of life?*
4. *How will my victory impact others?*

The Humble Way: On our own, we're no match for the enemy of our souls. But in Christ, we are more than conquerors. What we know about Him now pales in comparison to what He wants us to know of Him! Oh, the love, the majesty, and the power of the living God—the One who established the heavens and the One who brings life to everything He created! The more we know of Him, the stronger we grow in Him. We live in a day when people are in love with their own opinions and think they know more than they do. To be mighty in battle is to acknowledge that there's much we do not know. And that's okay, because we know the One who does know. Francis Frangipane writes,

> Only Jesus died for our sins; our pursuit of *Him* must become the singular goal of our spiritual endeavors.
>
> You must develop such a listening ear that the Spirit could speak to you anywhere about anything. Honor Him, and He will honor you. Keep the Word in your heart, and He will establish you in holiness before God. He will keep your way pure.[6]

Pause here. Try kneeling if you're able. Open your hands in your lap. And ask God to show you great and mighty things that you do not know (see Jeremiah 33:3). Wait quietly before Him and ask Him to speak to your heart. Write down your thoughts.

Discern the Fiery Arrows: We've visited this story previously in this book, but let's take a deeper look. In Luke's gospel, chapter eight, we read about a time Jesus told the disciples to get in the boat so they could cross to the other side of the Sea of Galilee. But once they were in the boat, a fierce storm arose. The Amplified version describes the storm as a severe gale of wind sweeping down as in a wind tunnel. The Sea of Galilee was surrounded by mountains, so the wind tunnel–like storms were always a threat. Yet Jesus slept in the storm. The disciples cried out to Jesus: Don't you care that we're about to drown? Jesus asked them, "Where is your faith?" What should the disciples have done? Wasn't calling on Jesus precisely what they should have done? I believe so. Or they could have rebuked the winds and waves themselves since earlier in the gospel we read that Jesus gave them power over the enemy. There's much about this story we could ponder. But the two things that surfaced for the disciples during this storm were (1) fear, and (2) the question of whether God cared. Jesus told them they were headed to the other side. But when the squall hit, they doubted what they'd

149

heard. Spend some time with God here and identify a storm in your life where these two things surfaced. Have you reconciled your fears and questions with God's love and faithfulness? Write out your thoughts.

_____

_____

_____

_____

_____

_____

Read the following passage and overlay it with your storm. Write out a faith-filled prayer telling your soul and God what's true about Him—He is good, kind, present, and faithful.

> The LORD directs the steps of the godly.
> He delights in every detail of their lives.
>
> Psalm 37:23

Say NO! One of the best ways to push back on the enemy is to pray God's Word and say it aloud. Spend some time saying and praying the passage below. Pray it and say it until you're able to believe it and receive it as the unwavering truth of Scripture:

> I can do all things [which He has called me to do] through Him who strengthens and empowers me [to fulfill His purpose—I am self-sufficient in Christ's sufficiency; I am ready for anything and equal

to anything through Him who infuses me with inner strength and confident peace.]

Philippians 4:13 AMP

Say YES! Prayerfully ask God to show you if you've given up any land to the enemy. Sometimes we wave the white flag of surrender because we're weary in battle. Other times we don't realize that something is ours, so we don't notice when the enemy takes it from us. And still other times, he steals our destiny, influence, and capacity for kingdom work by distracting us with worldly pursuits that seem enticing but will pass away when the earth passes away. Ask the Lord to show you the land He has for you. I love this verse below because I can picture myself looking for evidence of the enemy's occupation and finding him completely gone. And I can see myself enjoying an abundance of peace where there once were thickets and thorns and heartbreak. Prayerfully consider this verse and then journal your thoughts.

> A little while, and the wicked will be no more;
>   though you look for them, they will not be found.
> But the meek will inherit the land
>   and enjoy peace and prosperity.
>
> Psalm 37:10–11 NIV

Personalized Prayer

Mighty King Jesus,

I humble myself before You. Fill me afresh with the power of Your Spirit! Teach me to stand on Your Word with the kind of faith I've not known before. Help me to discern enemy schemes before they ever reach me. I'm done with being battered by my fears. Give me a fresh revelation of Your perfect love, which casts out all fear. These things I know to be true: You are good. You are faithful. And You will keep Your Word to me! Give me a vision for where You're taking me and what You want to accomplish in me. Put Your fire in my bones and Your passion in my heart. Help me run this race to win because I am on the winning side. In Your precious name, I pray. Amen.

Spiritual Intelligence Training
THIS IS WHY WE FIGHT!

1. Picture a spacious valley. The Philistine army gathers on one side, preparing for war. King Saul counters that move by assembling his army on the opposite hill. They face off, each waiting for the other to make the first move. Then Goliath steps out from the ranks of the Philistines to taunt the Israelites. He struts and swaggers and dares anyone to fight him. Saul and his men tremble in fear. Read 1 Samuel 17:1–11 and consider Goliath's question (v. 8): *Why even fight?* That question didn't originate from Goliath, but rather from Satan. He has spewed that question for generations. *Why. Even. Bother?* A legitimate question given the delays we as God's people so often face. He takes His time to bring the prodigal home, heal a marriage, or transform a community. Consider this face-off between Goliath and God's people and answer the following questions:

   a. Why did the Israelites need to fight this battle?

   b. Why do you need to fight your battles? What's at stake?

2. David's father sent him to the front lines with food gifts and to get a report on how his brothers were doing. But as soon as David arrived, he picked up on the bigger story at play. For forty days, Goliath strutted and taunted the Israelites. Imagine! Read 1 Samuel 17:12–27 and focus on this line from verse 26: "Who is this pagan Philistine anyway, that he is allowed to defy the armies of the living God?" How is David's perspective more accurate than that of the scared Israelites? Explain.

3. When it came time for David to go to battle, he already had it settled in his mind that Goliath wasn't defying him. He was fighting God Himself. David saw himself as part of the heavenly army and refused to be singled out by a foul-mouthed giant. In what ways has the enemy poked at you personally in hopes that you'll shrink back in fear or defeat?

4. Few Christians are willing to go the distance in battle. Why? Mainly because of fear, spiritual apathy, or self-protection. So when one

rises up to face his giant, others jealously pick him apart. Read 1 Samuel 17:28–29 and notice how David's brother accused David of things he himself was guilty of. When it's time for you to step up with fierce faith, will you be content to be misunderstood? Write down your thoughts.

5. Read 1 Samuel 17:32–39, where David recounts his past victories to King Saul. Notice how David's confidence in God soared with each victory God had given him. After reading this passage, answer the following questions:

   a. Which of your victories has strengthened your confidence in God?

   b. David realized he couldn't fight while wearing Saul's armor. How does this part of the story speak to you? Has someone offered you armor that doesn't fit you? Write down your thoughts.

6. David decided to rely on the way God had trained him in past battles. But imagine this scene—armies on opposite sides of the valley. One side is trembling in fear. The other side is sneering and taunting. Then out comes a young boy with a sling and a few stones. Read 1 Samuel 17:40–50. Once again, notice how Goliath tried to make it personal, but David didn't take the bait. In what predictable ways does the enemy taunt or insult you every time you decide to take your stand in faith?

7. Let's look at David's incredible response to Goliath: "You come to me with sword, spear, and javelin, but I come to you in the name of the LORD of Heaven's Armies—the God of the armies of Israel, whom you have defied. Today the LORD will conquer you, and I will kill you and cut off your head. . . . And the whole world will know that there is a God in Israel! And everyone assembled here will know that the LORD rescues His people, but not with sword and spear. This is the LORD's battle, and he will give you to us!"

   a. The Lord rescues His people. Did you need to hear that today? There is a day ahead when the Lord will make Himself known

154

on your battlefield, and He'll win a sound victory on your behalf. If you wanted to encourage a dear friend in your situation,
what would you say? Stay the course, my friend. Victory is up
ahead.

b. If that same friend asked you today, "Why even fight this battle?" how would you answer?

EIGHT

Guard Your Heart

Stay Engaged

That is your new identity. You are a son or daughter of God. You are
a child of the King. You are written into God's will, and you are an
heir of everything God has. You are a beneficiary of the lavish love
of God, which has changed you from failure to family. Grace not
only cancels guilt and shame; grace redefines you. You are a beloved
family member of God, and because of that you are given a seat at
the table with Almighty God.[1]

I had a vivid dream about fifteen years ago that I still remember
today. I've struggled my whole life with sleep issues. I rarely fall
into such a deep sleep that I dream, not to mention a dream that
serves as a jarring wake-up call. For the sake of analogy, I'll expand
on the idea of the dream with a little more detail.

Picture the following scene unfolding as you watch from above.
Battalions of soldiers are assigned to their posts. All troops are sent
to the front lines to push back enemy forces and gain ground in the
war. All but one group. This particular battalion was stationed in a
remote area, away from the front lines in a heavily wooded forest.
Their instructions were to set up base camp, practice their drills, keep

their weapons cleaned and ready to use, stand guard, stay alert, and *allow no intruders*. That was it. In due time they'd trade spots with another battalion and they needed to be battle ready.

At first, they did exactly as they were instructed. The soldiers built several sturdy blockade walls. They sparred with each other and practiced hand-to-hand combat. They ran through agility drills with ferocity. They checked their weapons daily. They stayed fit and kept an eye on things outside the perimeter. Eventually, though, they couldn't see the point of it all. The troops lost focus and let their guard down.

One day, while the soldiers all sat sleepily up against a circle of trees, a little girl wandered into camp. Grateful to have something to do, they gave her a snack and kicked a ball back and forth. Eventually, her mother came looking for her little girl. She repeatedly thanked the soldiers for their kindness. She then invited them back to her village for a meal as her way of saying thank you.

The soldiers looked at each other, shrugged their shoulders, and said, "Sure. Why not?" And what a great time they had, sitting around the bonfire with their new friends. They didn't think twice about leaving their equipment, supplies, and intel back at camp.

Visits to the village became a regular occurrence. Several times, over decadent meals, the village people asked their new friends to tell them stories of their military exploits. They jumped right in with tales of intrigue and danger, and they added a little embellishment here and there. The soldiers frequently overate, drank too much, stayed up too late, and slept in too long. They enjoyed the revelry but felt sluggish during the day. It didn't seem to matter, though, because they were not aware of any impending threat.

One day, the local women asked if they could wash the soldiers' uniforms and offered them civilian clothing to wear in the meantime. The soldiers happily accepted, were grateful for the help, and when the day was done, headed back to base camp dressed like the village people. Over the next few days, the women offered one reason after another why they didn't have their uniforms ready. The soldiers trusted their new friends and, frankly, weren't too worried about it.

Several days passed before the soldiers realized they hadn't heard from any of the locals. No visits. No children. No invitations to dinner. They decided to scope out the village, only to find it emptied and abandoned. Curious, they headed back to their spot in the woods. By the time the soldiers-turned-civilians returned to their base camp, they were under fire and totally unprepared. In a matter of minutes, the whole base camp and all its soldiers were lost.

What the soldiers never realized was that the village people were planted by the enemy. Their assignment was to infiltrate the camp and lure the soldiers into a passive, distracted state so the enemy could take them out when the time was right. These unarmed village people walked right onto a military base camp and found no resistance whatsoever. Why? Because the soldiers minimized the importance of their assignment. And since the soldiers felt no immediate consequence for their passivity, they were convinced they weren't vulnerable.

Apathy/Passivity:

- Puts us at risk (because it makes us vulnerable to enemy distractions).
- Puts others at risk (because we leave undone what ought to be done).
- Causes spiritual atrophy (as our spiritual muscles go flabby from lack of engagement).

Apathy is a lack of interest, enthusiasm, or concern for the things that matter deeply to God. Passivity is acceptance of what happens without active resistance, no matter the cost to the individual or to God's greater purposes on the earth. Apathy and passivity are the antitheses of kingdom life.

Apathy sets in when we think too much of ourselves (our comforts, conveniences, and preferences) and not enough of God and of His heart for the world. Passivity sets in when we think too little of ourselves and our calling. Passivity urges us to take the path of least resistance because we don't think we can do hard things. But we can. And we must.

When we so distance ourselves from God's heartbeat for the world that we overindulge to the point of apathy, the enemy infiltrates our camp and sets us up for failure. Passivity also paves the way for enemy invasion because we place a higher value on comfort in the moment than on the God-given purpose for our lives. We trade our birthright for a bowl of soup.[2]

God calls us to diligently guard our yard (our heart) from all kinds of toxic influences, and many books have been written on that topic. But I don't think we pay enough attention to the cost of apathy and passivity. Probably because, as with the soldiers in my dream, we don't feel the consequences right away.

> Therefore take up the whole armor of God, that you may be able to withstand in the evil day, and having done all, to stand.
>
> Ephesians 6:13 NKJV

The word *withstand* is translated from the Greek *anthistemi*. "The verb suggests vigorously opposing, bravely resisting, standing face-to-face against an adversary, standing your ground. Just as an antihistamine puts a block on histamine, anthistemi tells us that with the authority and spiritual weapons granted to us we can withstand evil forces."[3]

➤

Another security breach that keeps us from being valiant in battle is insecurity. If we consider our status in the kingdom an on-again, off-again proposition—if the circumstances around us and the circles of power before us carry more weight than Jesus' declaration that we're seated with Him—we will be easy and predictable prey for the enemy. Imagine yourself knowing so well how secure you are in

Passivity urges us to take the path of **least** resistance because we don't think we can do **hard** things. But we can. And we **must**.

Christ Jesus that you, like the apostle Paul, could stand before people of power with deep confidence and conviction.

Picture yourself around people who normally make you negatively self-aware because they excel where you don't, and envision yourself feeling joyful, assured, and called to stand wherever God places you. Your goal isn't to be popular, or even to be loved. You're already loved. And divinely equipped. Your goal is to walk into the territory God assigns you and to do so with God-given authority, power, love, and humility. People can react or think what they want. You're on mission and you've got heaven on your side.

Who doesn't prefer a time of ease over intense seasons of battle? But what we so often fail to realize is how powerfully God is using our current struggle to train us, refine us, and prepare us for the good, redemptive work He has for us ahead. He uses every twist and turn of our story. You have a spiritual agility and sharpness about you that is a direct result of the challenges you've faced. Your battle—though fierce and heartbreaking at times—has served you well, even if you can't see it at the moment.

Our enemy is on a short leash. The sooner we realize that there's a purpose in every battle and that we are on the winning side, the more confident in God's character we'll become and the more equipped for the battle we'll be.

> For who is God, but the LORD?
> Or who is a rock, except our God,
>
> The God who encircles me with strength
> And makes my way blameless?
>
> He makes my feet like hinds' feet [able to stand firmly and
>   tread safely on paths of testing and trouble];
> He sets me [securely] upon my high places.
>
> He trains my hands for war,
> So that my arms can bend a bow of bronze.

You have also given me the shield of Your salvation,
And Your right hand upholds and sustains me;
Your gentleness [Your gracious response when I pray] makes
  me great.

You enlarge the path beneath me and make my steps secure,
So that my feet will not slip.

Psalm 18:31–36 AMP

God will sometimes allow an overplayed enemy attack to position us for freedom. He knows what He has imparted to us. He knows what's in us (the power of His own Son!), and He sees who we can be when we learn to walk in the resurrection power made available to us. I cannot tell you how many times I've looked over my shoulder at the battles I've faced only to realize that those very battles protected me from something far worse than what I was enduring. How? My trials put me on guard, kept me alert, and compelled me to be deeply dependent on God. Plus, I came through each hardship with a firmer grasp of His Word and more profound confidence in His character. Our battles keep us spiritually fit, alert, and engaged.

Consider King David. He was at his best when his current battle compelled him to be deeply dependent on God. He was at his worst when he chose ease over engagement. His spiritual apathy cost him and others greatly.[4]

Times of ease can be a sweet relief and a gift from God, but we must never confuse God-given rest with self-imposed spiritual apathy. Don't think for a moment that just because you're enjoying a time of rest, the enemy is on a beach somewhere enjoying himself too. We often let our guard down during times of ease, and that's when the enemy gets away with what he shouldn't.

You're in the Center of God's Circle

When I was in high school, I was a varsity cheerleader, a homecoming princess, and a gymnast. But due to some childhood trauma

163

Your **goal** is to walk into the territory God **assigns** you and to do so **with** God-given authority, power, love, and humility.

that I suffered at the hands of a few teenage boys, I was also painfully insecure. I couldn't find my footing to save my life. You'd find me on the sidelines at the varsity football games with the popular cheerleaders, but I wasn't a legitimate member of their group. They didn't care for me much. But I don't fault them for that because I didn't care for me much either.

The sense of being outside the circle followed me into adulthood. I believed a lie about my value and my place in the world. Whenever a group of popular people made plans without me, it confirmed my inner bias that I simply didn't belong. And when I was invited to participate, it didn't register at all with my soul because the imposter syndrome compelled me to believe they were mistaken to pick me.

One day I cried out in prayer to God, knowing I had a flawed view of myself but at a loss for what to do about it. The Lord whispered to my heart, *Susie, you've felt outside the circle your whole life, but that circle is actually an illusion. It has no value in heaven.* Then I pictured Him drawing a circle around me when He whispered, *You're inside my circle, and that's the only one that matters.* The truth settled into my soul that day.

How many people go through life thinking themselves outside a circle that holds no value in heaven? What would change for them if they understood and embraced their place at the table of grace? What if they genuinely saw themselves as the apple of God's eye?

Over and over again, God upsets the status quo. He purposely chooses the weak, the outcast, and the marginal for His great purposes.

Read this powerful passage:

Remember, dear brothers and sisters, that few of you were wise in the world's eyes or powerful or wealthy when God called you. Instead, God chose things the world considers foolish in order to shame those who think they are wise. And he chose things that are powerless to shame those who are powerful. God chose things despised by the

Over and over again, God **upsets** the status quo. He **purposely** chooses the weak, the outcast, and the marginal for His **great** purposes.

world, things counted as nothing at all, and used them to bring to nothing what the world considers important. As a result, no one can ever boast in the presence of God.

1 Corinthians 1:26–29

No one can touch God's glory. There's no Hollywood superstar, big-tech giant, multibillionaire, or political hard hitter who wouldn't utterly fall apart in God's presence apart from His amazing grace. It's almost laughable how much we as human beings posture for position when any position apart from being seated with Christ is simply a house of cards.

Though social hierarchy on the earth is a thing, and though privileged circles within various people groups exist, we must not let earthly value systems dictate our perspective on our own value or our mission in the world. Those spheres of importance matter only so far as they serve God's purposes. They have no power to validate who God has already established that we are.

God consistently uses people who seem to be outside the circle, and He seems to love to do so. He takes regular, flawed, weak people and positions them to interrupt the enemy's plans and establish His ultimate purposes on the earth.

- Joseph was an outsider, as far as his brothers were concerned. Then he became an insider in Egypt. God promoted him and positioned him to save a nation. (See Genesis 50.)
- Moses was an insider (raised by Egyptians), but God called him to be an outsider and align with his people (at a significant cost), so he could lead them out of captivity and into freedom. (Read the book of Exodus.)
- David was an outsider (his own father didn't even consider calling him in from the fields when the prophet Samuel arrived to anoint the future king), but God raised him up to be an insider—He crowned David king and called him to

conquer the Israelites' enemies. (Read 1 Samuel 16 through 2 Samuel 8.)

- Esther was an outsider (a Jewish girl) raised up to be an insider (queen), and God used her to save her people. (Read the book of Esther.)
- Rahab was an outsider (a Gentile prostitute), and God moved on her faith, used her to save a couple of Jewish spies, and grafted her into the lineage of Christ. (Read Joshua 2.)
- Ruth was an outsider (a Moabite), and God brought her inside first through her risky faith and deep commitment to her mother-in-law, and then through her marriage to Boaz. God grafted her into the lineage of Christ. (Read the book of Ruth.)
- Jesus was an insider (seated in heaven, one with God and the Holy Spirit) and stepped down from His throne to enter the womb of a teenage girl. He, who knew no sin, became sin so that we could become the righteousness of God through Him. He became an outsider so that we who bear His name would become insiders—heirs to the kingdom, filled with His Spirit, assigned to carry out His purposes on the earth. Hallelujah! (Read the Gospels.)
- Paul was an insider (a Roman citizen and a terrorist-Pharisee), and God knocked him off his horse, called him to be an outsider; he followed Jesus and walked with those he'd once terrorized, and God used him to change the world. (Read Acts 9.)

Over and over again, we see that God uses those outside the proverbial circle to do His best work. Often, there's a hierarchy within the circle that's in direct conflict with the Christlike way. So when God does intend to use someone within the circle, He first calls them out of the established system; He leads them through a breaking-humbling process; He builds them back up again, and then works through them in ways that make history.

Maybe the idea of being an outsider has never bothered you or occurred to you. If so, that's wonderful. But allow me to push back just a little bit. Sometimes, when people say, "I really don't care what people think of me," they do so from a place of pride, rebellion, or independence. Often, such attitudes are born out of a wounded, unhealed heart. But if left unattended, hearts harden and love grows cold. Self-preservation is not the same as guarding your heart with all diligence. Isolation is not conducive to living in the world and loving others with a pure heart.

A mature kingdom person is wise to attitudes that spoil joy and diminish love. They see their heart as a sacred place where the Spirit dwells. They are quick to shut down thoughts and feelings that conflict with life and peace. They're engaged with others—even difficult people—but they're intimately connected to God and take their cues from Him. This person might say something like, *"I love and care about you. I'll even take risks with you. You have the power to hurt me, but you don't have the power to diminish my value or make me doubt who I am. Jesus has already established that for me."*

There's a tender toughness in the heart of the believer. Consider Paul. He at one point said that it mattered very little what others thought of him (see 1 Corinthians 4:3), but he also said he'd give up his own salvation for others to know Christ (see Romans 9:3). This is a man in whom Christ had so increased that he ultimately died to the fear of man. Paul lived fully alive in the love Christ had for him and others.

Maybe you don't resonate with being inside or outside the circle, but you're aware of the nuanced ways the enemy works to poke at your wounds, confirm rejection, and push you off your game. To grow in maturity is to learn to quickly separate the people the enemy uses (sometimes he painfully uses those closest to you) from the message the enemy is trying to confirm in you. Use every one of these battles as an opportunity to pursue deeper healing in Jesus and to become proficient at wielding your sword and your shield and shut down the enemy's lies before they have a chance to take root in your soul. Stand firm against the enemy. Stay tender before God. You are a miracle in the making.

Prayerful Reflective Questions

1. *Lord, have I let my guard down? Have I allowed my passions for the things You care about to diminish?*
2. *In what ways has the enemy had consistent access to me? What's the best way for me to shut him down?*
3. *Is there any root of rejection still at work within me?*
4. *Are there unhealed places within me that I'm unaware of?*

The Humble Way: We don't often imagine that apathy, passivity, or rejection will hinder the work of God in our midst. But they do, significantly so. Yet when we remember how profoundly loved we are, how astoundingly called and equipped we are, and how unfathomably covered we are, we'll begin to dream with God about the impossible things He wants to do in and through us. Not from a "make me great" mindset, but from a humble, daring, "I'm shaking in my boots but I know this will please You" mind-

170

set. Consider Jabez's prayer below, and then write out your own audacious, faith-filled prayer.

> There was a man named Jabez who was more honorable than any of his brothers. His mother named him Jabez because his birth had been so painful. He was the one who prayed to the God of Israel, "Oh, that you would bless me and expand my territory! Please be with me in all that I do and keep me from all trouble and pain!" And God granted him his request.
>
> 1 Chronicles 4:9–10

Discern the Fiery Arrows: I imagine that most of us sometimes feel like outsiders in one way or another. I feel like an outsider because of the health challenges I've battled my whole adult life. I'm surrounded by healthy people who don't even think about how they'll sleep tonight or how they'll feel in the morning. It takes incredible mental fortitude to stay out of the comparison ditch. How about you? Maybe you have a prodigal who's breaking your heart. You were an intentional and good parent, yet they wandered. You live with a broken heart, continually bleeding under your armor. Or maybe your struggle is in marriage, or finances, or your weight, or your job, or your house. Others have what you long for, and they seem to come by it with ease, without struggle. What's that thing for you? Let's do two things right now. Let's identify the lie behind the heartbreak. And in a moment, we'll reaffirm our trust in God.

Hope deferred makes the heart sick,
but a longing fulfilled is a tree of life.

Proverbs 13:12 NIV

Spend a few moments with God and pour out your heart to Him. Be honest about your heartbreak and about the longings of your heart. Lament is a sacred and vital practice. As Kyle Strobel said on my show one day, prayer is "a place to be honest and a place to be known."[5] Write out your prayer.

Say NO! Pause here and consider how the enemy might be trying to leverage your heartbreak in a way that turns your heart away from God or that makes you believe wrongly about Him. Your Father is not holding out on you! He has good things planned for you. And He promises to redeem every single aspect of your story. Write out a faith declaration that looks something like this:

In the name of Jesus, I declare that my God is for me, not against me!

Devil, I refuse to listen to your lies another day. I command you to shut your mouth and leave my presence. You have no authority to enter this space and no right to lie to me. I shut down this dialogue immediately and refuse to take the bait. In the name of Jesus, be gone! And heavenly Father, I declare that You are good.

Your promises are true. And You are working in ways that will one day take my breath away. I love You. I will trust You, Lord. Amen.

Say YES! The opposites of apathy, passivity, and rejection are *engagement* and *belonging*. God invites us to trust Him more today than we did yesterday! To fan into flame the gift of God within us. And to pursue Him so earnestly that our heart begins to beat in rhythm with His. He intends for us to go from strength to strength, glory to glory, shining ever brighter until the full light of day! Two of the many benefits of the kingdom are authority over all the power of the enemy (Luke 10:19), and the promise of abundant life even in the middle of our war (John 10:10). But neither of these things just happens for us apart from us. We have authority over worry, despair, and discouragement, but we have to exercise authority. We are promised an overflowing life, but we have to contend for it. Read the following verse and consider how the enemy has baited you into apathy (so he can steal from you) and/or rejection (so you'll be tied up with negative self-awareness and not dare to take back from the enemy that which belongs to you).

> The thief comes only in order to steal and kill and destroy. I came that they may have and enjoy life, and have it in abundance [to the full, till it overflows].
>
> John 10:10 AMP

173

Don't skim over this one. Give God some time and space to search your heart and show you things that perhaps you cannot see on the surface. Remember, though God leads us into seasons of rest after intense seasons of battle, we easily blur the lines and find ourselves disengaged from all God wants to accomplish in and through us. Think of it this way: Would you say you were more involved in kingdom work in seasons past than you are now? Why is that? Ask the Lord to speak to your heart. Also, when the enemy gets away with pushing our rejection button (but we fail to recognize it), we default to solutions that only feed the lie (we eat, drink, buy, hang with people who don't challenge us, etc.). But when we see the flaming arrow for what it is, we're more apt to raise our shield in defense and then raise our sword in offense! Whenever, through an enemy attack, we become aware of our limitations, we need only to run to Jesus and say, "Expand Your kingdom in and through me!" And He will. What is God stirring in you right now? Write down your thoughts.

Personalized Prayer

Heavenly Father,

I love You! Awaken fresh faith in me! Forgive me for the ways I've allowed apathy to lull me into caring more about my comfort than I do about Your kingdom. Stir up a passion in my soul, Lord! It's time for the church to engage, and I know You are calling me to more than I can imagine. In Your name, I reject rejection and accept acceptance. I refuse apathy, and I embrace engagement. Give me a fresh vision for where You are taking me and put fierce faith in me to follow You there. I will guard my heart with all diligence, and I trust You to establish me in Your purposes for me. In Your Son's name, I pray. Amen.

Spiritual Intelligence Training
STAY MOBILIZED

1. *Immobilization* is the act of or the resulting state of *preventing someone or something from moving or operating as intended.* This is what the enemy is always after in our lives. He aims to steal, kill, and destroy, but always to hinder God's miraculous and breathtaking work in and through us. He uses obstacles, delays, difficult people, sickness, and nitpicky harassment, to name a few tactics. Read John 10:10 in the Amplified version and consider:

   a. What have been the greatest hindrances to the abundant life Jesus talked about here?

   b. In what ways have you pushed back on the enemy of your soul? In what ways have you allowed him to get away with too much in your life?

2. Nehemiah was a man of conviction. He saw beyond his personal comforts to the more significant story God was writing during his day. Read Nehemiah 1 and write your thoughts on the following points:

   a. Notice the order of Nehemiah's prayer (declaration of God's faithfulness, recognition of Israel's sin, a reminder of His promises, and an appeal for intervention). Using that same model, write out a prayer for your nation.

   b. Nehemiah's heart was tied to the condition of his people. One way the enemy immobilizes us is to get us so wrapped up in our personal story that it doesn't occur to us to carry a burden for God's people. No matter where you find yourself today, ask God to burden your heart for what burdens His. Write down your prayer.

3. When God gives a vision, He makes provision. Read Nehemiah 2 and notice how God not only opened wide the doors of opportunity, but He also provided all Nehemiah would need for the journey. Still, Nehemiah faced opposition. Just as David relied on the God of Angel

Armies for success, Nehemiah also declared, "The God of heaven will help us succeed."

    a. If you could do anything at all for God, what would it be?

    b. What kinds of opposition might you face?

    c. Do you tend to rely more on your strength or God's faithfulness? Be honest. ☺

    d. How is this current battle training you to trust God more than you trust yourself?

4. Let's look at some of the opposition Nehemiah faced and see what we can learn from it. Read Nehemiah 4:1–3, and once again (much like the face-off between David and Goliath), you see God's enemies hurling personal insults at God's people. Sanballat was so angry he flew into a rage. What a picture of the enemy's temper when we dare to forge ahead despite attempts to derail us. Sit with this passage for a moment. When you stand fast in faith, when you decide to keep going, when you determine to trust God for another day, your enemy flies into a rage. How does that idea impact you?

5. Read Nehemiah 4:4–10 and remember, we all get weary in battle sometimes. That's why the world needs more prophetic encouragers and leaders like Nehemiah. Whom do you need to encourage today? Somebody is weary in battle and needs a fresh word from you.

6. Read Nehemiah 4:11–20 and notice how Nehemiah stepped up with a new strategy in response to the increased opposition. He knew this project wasn't just about building a city wall; it was about the future of God's people. He said, "Don't be afraid of the enemy! Remember the Lord, who is great and glorious, and fight for your brothers, your sons, your daughters, your wives, and your homes!" When the enemy opposition is heating up around you, ask God if you need a new strategy to stand, stay engaged, and trust Him to deliver you.

7. Do you have a clear picture of the legacy God wants to leave through you? If yes, write it down. What kind of legacy do you want to leave? If you don't know, ask God to give you a grander view of your life's story and its importance.

NINE

Contend for the Promises

Stay Fierce

———

One day, we won't need to trust his love any longer, because we'll be in the presence of our One Great Love. After endless years of trying to see Him through the haze and mystery of life's unanswerable questions, we'll finally see him as he's always seen us—face-to-face. On that day, suffering, tears, death, and mystery itself will be no more. The long journey will be over. At last, sons and daughters of God, we'll be . . . home.[1]

Our kids were young when I first contracted Lyme disease. One day, I had a doctor's appointment, but none of my regular baby-sitters were available. So a friend of a friend had a friend, whose daughter happened to be available to sit that day. We lived on a cul-de-sac, which was great, but it backed up to a fifty-mile-an-hour road. There was no fence between our neighbor's backyard and that busy road. My boys were one, three, and five years old at the time. My middle son, Luke, was our strong-willed child and kept us on our toes.

After my appointment, I pulled into the cul-de-sac and noticed the baby-sitter pushing Jordan around in the stroller while our oldest son, Jake, pushed his little lawnmower around the front yard. I didn't see Luke anywhere. I pulled into the driveaway, and the sitter cheerfully greeted me. "Hey! How'd it go?" I looked around the yard and between the houses and said, "Good. Where's Luke?" She looked over her shoulder, shrugged, and said (and I kid you not), "Um. I don't know. He was just too hard to keep track of." True story. I panicked and said, "*What?!* Where is he? When did you last see him?" I took off running around the houses that backed up to the highway and found my chubby three-year-old sitting on the ground—about fifty feet from the highway—pulling up fistfuls of grass and watching the tiny blades flutter to the ground. I scooped him up in my arms, buried my face in his neck, and thanked Jesus for his safety. No wonder this sitter had no other gigs on her calendar.

Luke is now an oak of righteousness. He is a man of God, an amazing husband, and an honorable son. He loves God's Word, is as humble as they come, and his excellence and work ethic mirror his father's ways. We couldn't love him more if we tried. When he graduated from high school, he said to us, "Mom, Dad, I know I was a bit of a handful when I was young. But you never made me feel like the problem child. You always challenged me to believe that I was made for better things than I could see at the time. Thank you." We can all be a bit of a handful at times. But when God looks at us, He sees beauty, potential, and great worth.

I tell you that story to say that Luke was worth the effort we put into training him, raising him, correcting him, and redirecting him. We saw great potential in him. And it's the same with us. Your life—the life God promised and intended for you—*is worth the effort*. There will be days when it feels easier to just let it all go and drift with the culture's current. There will be times when you're tempted to shrug your shoulders at your promised land because it feels too difficult to lay hold of or too far off to believe God for. But let me tell you something. If God promised it, it's worth the effort to lay hold of it.

I shudder to imagine if something had happened to Luke that day because the baby-sitter picked the easier path instead of the right one. The life Luke lives, the people he blesses, the fruit that comes from his walk with God have become realities because we fought for him when he was young and because he now contends for the promises of God in his own life. He'd tell you that as painful as the battles can sometimes be, they're worth the fight.

➤

Each day on my radio show, I start the conversation by asking my guests, "Is there a verse or passage from Scripture you've been pondering these days?" I love this question because God speaks to us through His Word. And so often, when my guests share their thoughts, it brings Scripture to life.

One day, author and pastor Allen Jackson joined me on the show. I asked him my opening question, and his answer cut me to the heart. Here's my paraphrase of his response as I remember it. He said, "Susie, I've been pondering the story from Scripture where Paul goes before Agrippa to testify about Jesus. Here Agrippa has the world's greatest evangelist in front of him, explaining who Jesus is, and in so many words, Agrippa responds, 'I was almost persuaded to become a Christian.'" Pastor Allen went on to say, "It made me wonder if there are areas in my own life where I'm only almost persuaded that what God says is true."

If I could have backed away from the mic and found a room to be in by myself, I would have broken down and cried. In fact, you can hear my voice crack on the air as I responded to his insights. I've walked through a neurological firestorm while writing this book. Some days I sit at my computer and pound out the words while surges of numbing and dizziness course through my body. Picture working on your laptop out in a hailstorm. That's what it has felt like.

Was I persuaded that God would heal me? Not really. Some days I had hope, but other days, not so much. Had I let go of some of the other promises I know He made to me? In what ways have I been wavering between two opinions? Have I been only almost persuaded that God is who He says He is and that He'll do what He says He'll do?

> If you need wisdom, ask our generous God, and he will give it to you. He will not rebuke you for asking. But when you ask him, be sure that your faith is in God alone. Do not waver, for a person with divided loyalty is as unsettled as a wave of the sea that is blown and tossed by the wind. Such people should not expect to receive anything from the Lord. Their loyalty is divided between God and the world, and they are unstable in everything they do.
>
> James 1:5–8

I realized that I'd been so battered by my battle that I'd lost my roar. And I don't think I'm the only one. We've all been through a lot in the past couple of years. Many of us have lost our roar. We waver back and forth and wonder:

- *Is it really true that I'm NOT at the mercy of the times or man's opinions, or even my opinions of myself? Am I truly, deeply loved and secure in Christ Jesus?*
- *Is it really true that a healed, whole soul is my spiritual right as an heir of God?*
- *Is it really true that I have a unique and powerful call on my life—one that matters significantly in the greater kingdom story God is writing on the earth today?*
- *Is it really true that there are promises in Scripture for me? That, as I pray them, say them, and believe them, I WILL see mountains move and waters part?*

In 1 Kings chapter 18, Elijah asks the people, "How long will you waver between two opinions? If the LORD is God, trust Him! Believe Him!"[2]

How long *will* we waver between two opinions? Are there things we can absolutely, resolutely stand on and believe God for? I believe so! In fact, I'd say that for us to grow and mature, we must get to a

In what ways have
I been **wavering**
between two opinions?
Have I been only
almost **persuaded**
that God is who He
says He is and that
He'll do what He
says He'll do?

place where we can shout and declare, "I KNOW this is true! These things are mine because I am in Christ, and He is in me!"

Four Things That Are Yours

1. Identity/security
2. Healed and whole soul
3. Your calling
4. God's promise to empower you

We can personalize it this way. Shout it out loud until your soul knows it's true!

- *I'm secure!*
- *I'm healing!*
- *I'm called!*
- *I'm empowered!*

I Am Secure. I Am Loved.

These four things are promised to us as believers. But we have to contend for them. And it's not a one-and-done proposition. God wants us to grow into these realities with an ever-increasing capacity. For example, you're saved by grace, through faith, not of yourself; it's a gift from God, so no one can brag about their eternal security (see Ephesians 2:8–9, which we'll unpack in just a bit). So how do you grow in the reality of your salvation? You learn just what it is that Jesus accomplished on your behalf. You stay in awe that He saved you.

When the disciples returned from a ministry trip and marveled that the demons obeyed them, Jesus said, "Don't marvel that the demons obey you. Marvel that your name is written in the Book of Life"[3] (my paraphrase). As powerful as it is to see demons flee, more phenomenal still is the fact that God rescued you from the kingdom of darkness and transferred you into the kingdom of His dear Son.[4] You couldn't cross that chasm yourself, so Jesus made a way and paid your way.

As you grow in your understanding of how much He loves you (though it's so great you won't fully understand it),[5] you'll find yourself more and more at home in God's presence—increasingly confident of His character. You'll be sturdier in your faith and more assured of your place at the table of grace.

Too many Christians pray the salvation prayer and don't think much more about the stunning, powerful reality of what they've just inherited. The more you grow, the more you know that you are loved and secure, and nothing—and no one—can snatch you out of God's hand.[6]

> When I think of all this, I fall to my knees and pray to the Father, the Creator of everything in heaven and on earth. I pray that from his glorious, unlimited resources he will empower you with inner strength through his Spirit. Then Christ will make his home in your hearts as you trust in him. Your roots will grow down into God's love and keep you strong. And may you have the power to understand, as all God's people should, how wide, how long, how high, and how deep his love is. May you experience the love of Christ, though it is too great to understand fully. Then you will be made complete with all the fullness of life and power that comes from God.
>
> Ephesians 3:14–19

Brain scientist Dr. Tim Jennings issued this challenge to my listeners one day: If you spend fifteen minutes a day pondering the love God has for you, it'll literally change your brain structure, and it'll change your life.[7]

God's love is so great that we can never fully grasp it this side of heaven. Knowing this love in increasing measures is what grounds us in the things of God, answers those nagging questions about our identity, and heals the inner wounds that lie beneath the surface. So why *wouldn't* we actively engage with God, recapture our roar, and seek to understand this love in increasing measures *with all our heart?*

No matter how long you've walked with God, there's always far more of Him to know and experience. It's like we're standing on the beach holding a Dixie cup while the endless ocean waters roar in front of us. Insecurity for the believer is an illusion. We may feel insecure at times, but we never really are insecure. We're seated with Christ, after all.

Maybe this declaration will fuel your fire:

In the name of Jesus,
I reject rejection!
I accept acceptance!
I reject insecurity!
I embrace holy confidence!
I reject fear!
I embrace perfect love!
I am in Christ; Christ is in me; I lack NO good thing!

After walking with God for many years, spending ample time in His presence, and familiarizing myself with passages from Scripture that speak of God's love, I can shout with certainty, "I KNOW that I am loved! I KNOW that I am secure in Him! And nothing can separate me from His love!" Yet even now, I can tell that I've only touched the edges of what God is really like. One day we'll see Him face-to-face.

> Dear friends, we are already God's children, but he has not yet shown us what we will be like when Christ appears. But we do know that we will be like him, for we will see him as he really is.
>
> 1 John 3:2

With identity comes certain privileges. And with privilege comes responsibility. There's a world of lost people out there who have no idea how much God loves them.

Insecurity for the believer is an **illusion**. We may feel insecure at times, but we **never** really are insecure. We're **seated** with Christ, after all.

I Am Healing

Anybody who knows me knows I'm very disciplined, and I've had to be, given the health challenges I face. But I also enjoy a disciplined life. I worked in the fitness industry for many years and love to live with a healthy mindset. But this recent battle has kicked my butt. None of my disciplines seemed to work or matter. I just kept getting worse. The neurological surges terrified me, and I was so disappointed that God continued to allow me to fight this battle after thirty years. One day He whispered to my heart, *Susie, you get a healthy life through stewardship. You get a healed life through faith.*

Now, I believe strongly that we need to partner with God on our journey to wholeness. We play a part, and He fulfills His role. And sometimes it's hard work. And yet, it's worth the fight. But I realized that my disappointment with God only increased with all of my strivings to stay on top of this illness. Striving in the flesh and experiencing God in the Spirit are incompatible. When we strive in the flesh, we'll blame God for not doing His part, when in fact, He's waiting for us to stop our striving so we can actually experience His power in the very places where our souls refused to rest.

> Be still and know (recognize, understand) that I am God.
> I will be exalted among the nations! I will be exalted in the earth.
>
> Psalm 46:10 AMP

Striving glorifies us. Knowing and experiencing God in the broken places of our lives glorifies Him. I don't know how or when I shifted from responsible stewardship to hyper-vigilant striving, but my frustration and hurt revealed that I'd lost my way. I marvel at the patience and kindness of God. I humbled myself before Him and asked for forgiveness. I longed to experience His power in the places of my striving. I felt the nudge to grab my Bible and do a word study on Ephesians 2:8–9 (NIV):

For it is by grace you have been saved, through faith—and this is not from yourselves, it is the gift of God—not by works, so that no one can boast.

The Greek word for "saved" in this passage is *sōzō*, which means to *save, heal, restore, make well, restore to health, to save from the penalties of judgment.* This is mind-boggling when you think of it! And proof that salvation isn't just a ticket to heaven; it's an invitation to saving grace and soul wholeness. Follow Jesus through the Gospels and you'll see a Savior who not only preached about the coming kingdom, but also continually addressed the human condition.

Think through this with me for a moment. I can get a healthy life through stewardship (which is essential), but I need a healed life—at a deep, soul level—and I can only acquire such a gift by faith. I can't buy it, bribe for it, earn it, or perform well enough for God to give it to me. By grace, through faith, I lay hold of a kind of wholeness I never dreamed possible.

My health battle has taken a toll on my soul. I need more than physical healing, and I have the sense that you do too. I know there are several different positions on whether or not such miracles happen today regarding physical healing. I write on this topic extensively in my book *Fully Alive: Learning to Flourish—Mind, Body, & Spirit.* But for the sake of the point I'm trying to make, let me unpack my thoughts on physical healing.

First and foremost, I'm a work in progress. I, like everyone else, see as in a glass dimly. And there are some things I just don't know or understand. That said, from my vantage point, based on what I read in Scripture (and the many verified documented cases on miracles), I believe with everything in me that God still heals today. My own son was miraculously healed from a serious back injury.

However, I have trouble with the mindset that says, "God always heals. No exceptions. If you don't get your miracle, that's on you." That seems like such a painful and condescending approach to the

Follow Jesus through the Gospels and you'll see a **Savior** who not only preached about the **coming** kingdom, but also continually **addressed** the human condition.

one who has already suffered so much. Jesus was moved with compassion when He saw the needs before Him. He said it only takes a mustard seed of faith to move mountains. And He continually met people where He found them. If, when you encounter the sufferer, your instinctive response is judgement and impatience (and not empathy and compassion), you're dealing in formulas, not in faith. Jesus was always moved by compassion.

I've known very godly people who've gotten sick and died, and who walked intimately with God up until their very last breath. I don't understand why God heals some and not others. But I do believe we would see more miracles on the earth if more of us believed that God was willing to intervene on our behalf in a miraculous way. But for now, I lean in to the mystery. And if I lean too heavily to one side, I want it to be on the side of faith. Until I take my last breath, I will pray this passage for myself and others and believe it with all of my heart:

> Praise the LORD, my soul;
>   all my inmost being, praise his holy name.
> Praise the LORD, my soul,
>   and forget not all his benefits—
> who forgives all your sins
>   and heals all your diseases,
> who redeems your life from the pit
>   and crowns you with love and compassion,
> who satisfies your desires with good things
>   so that your youth is renewed like the eagle's.
>   Psalm 103:1–5 NIV

In his brilliant book *Gentle and Lowly*, Dane Ortlund writes:

Jesus Christ's earthly ministry was one of giving back to undeserving sinners their humanity. We tend to think of the miracles of the Gospels as interruptions in the natural order. Yet German theologian

Jurgen Moltmann points out that miracles are not an interruption of the natural order but the restoration of the natural order. We are so used to a fallen world that sickness, disease, pain, and death seem natural. In fact, *they* are the interruption.[8]

> When Jesus expels demons and heals the sick, he is driving out of creation the powers of destruction, and is healing and restoring created beings who are hurt and sick. The lordship of God to which the healings witness, restores creation to health. Jesus' healings are not supernatural miracles in a natural world. They are the only truly "natural" thing in a world that is unnatural, demonized and wounded.[9]

Physical healing is one thing. But soul healing and restoration? Can we all jump in the deep end on this one? I know that God intends to restore our soul (Psalm 23) and that He wants us to live life abundantly (John 10:10), and He wants to show us His goodness in the land of the living (Psalm 27:13). It is for freedom that Christ has set us free (Galatians 5:1)!

As has happened to me, your storms and battles have taken a toll on your soul. God wants to tend to those things for you. *By grace, through faith*, you are "sŏzō'd"—restored, made well, healed, and saved. Soul healing is part of your kingdom inheritance, and just because that kind of healing most often happens over time and in layers doesn't mean we should be passive about contending for the fullness of this promise. Imagine a healthier, healed you a year from now. What if God miraculously delivered you from:

- buried trauma
- disappointment
- heartbreak
- insecurity
- fear
- regret

- always bracing for impact
- isolation and self-protection

Can you shout with me from the housetops?
I am loved and secure!
I am healing!

I Am Called

For we are God's masterpiece. He has created us anew in Christ Jesus,
so we can do the good things he planned for us long ago.

Ephesians 2:10

I write about your God-given purpose and calling extensively in my
book *Your Beautiful Purpose*, but I want to borrow a point from
that message to help us better understand what God has called us
to. If you were to line up ten women on the stage, all would have a
calling as unique as they are. But these four directives apply to all
of us when it comes to our calling:

- Be much with God—*To make your walk with the Lord
  your highest priority, your greatest treasure, and your most
  grounding influence. To grow so acquainted with His voice
  that you listen when He speaks, and you do what He says.
  And best of all, you enjoy His presence because He greatly
  enjoys you.*
- Do the next thing He tells you to do—*As you walk with
  God and grow more in tune with His voice, just do the next
  things He says to do. If you do what He tells you to do
  today, you'll get where you need to be tomorrow.*
- Give Him access to your character and your story—*We cannot mature in the faith or lay hold of all He has for us apart
  from the refining, purifying work of God in our midst. When*

God puts His finger on something in our lives, we humbly respond. When He corrects, redirects, or convicts, we humbly respond. When He points out something that offends Him (Psalm 139), we humbly respond. He disciplines those He loves, and He's in the process of making us someone we never dreamed we could be. He's transforming us into His likeness. Imagine.

- (If you dare), ask Him to do the impossible in and through you—*Without faith, it's impossible to please God, and anyone who comes to Him must believe that He exists and that He rewards those who earnestly seek Him (see Hebrews 11:6). I dare you to ask Him regularly: Do the impossible in and through me, Lord! Then follow His lead.*

Shout it out with me:
I am loved and secure!
I am healing!
I am called!

I Am Empowered

When I considered Pastor Allen's thoughts on being *almost persuaded*, I started to think of some of the instances in Scripture where God's people were *fully* convinced that God had the power to do what He promised.

- Abraham was fully persuaded that God had the power to do what He promised. (See Romans 4.)
- Elijah was fully persuaded that God would show a wandering people that He was the One True God. (See 1 Kings 18.)
- Paul was fully persuaded that nothing could ever separate us from God's love. (See Romans 8.)
- Paul was fully persuaded that God was able to guard that which he entrusted to Him. (See 2 Timothy 1:12.)

Somehow, in some way, we've got to get to a point where we trust God's Word and His ways more than we trust our past experiences and our own perception of our current circumstances. God wants the eyes of our hearts to open up. He wants us to see things as they are and not as they seem.

Years ago, I spent an extensive time studying Romans 4, where we read about Abraham's great faith in the face of incredible odds. I wrote out this paraphrased prayer to encourage my own faith. I pray it encourages you today.

Without weakening in my faith,
> *I'll face the fact that there are many reasons*
> *I should not be able to fulfill the call of God on my life.*
> *But I will not waver in unbelief regarding the promises of God!*
> *No, I'll be strengthened in my faith, giving glory to God*
> *Because I am fully persuaded that GOD has the power*
> *To do what He promised.*
> *Therefore, I put no confidence in _____*
> *(fill in the blank: my weaknesses, my symptoms, my insecurities, my fears)*
> *Because I put all my hope in the power, authority, and faithfulness of almighty God*
> *Who daily establishes His purposes for me!*
> *Will you shout it out with me?*
> *I am loved and secure!*
> *I am healing!*
> *I am called!*
> *I am empowered!*

Prayerful Reflective Questions

1. *Lord, in which of these four areas do you want me to boldly engage my faith? (Loved and Secure, Healing, Called, Empowered)*
2. *In what ways have I believed wrongly about You and about this particular area of my life?*
3. *In what ways have I wavered between two opinions and been only almost persuaded that You'll be faithful?*
4. *Lord, will You give me a fresh revelation of the wonder of my salvation? Open my eyes to the wonder of what You did for me.*

The Humble Way: There's a big difference between presumptuously dictating to God (as if He's somehow bound to do what we say), and humbly declaring what's true about Him. Write out a two-part prayer. First, humble yourself before Him and give Him the honor He deserves. Then, write out a bold yet humble prayer, declaring God to be who He says He is. Declare His goodness over your circumstances.

Declare His concern over your affairs. And declare these truths: *I am loved! I am secure! I am healing! I am called! I am empowered!*

Discerning the Fiery Arrows: Sometimes the enemy attacks with a full-on frontal assault. You know it's him because you're suddenly derailed by discouragement, despair, or disappointment with God. But other times, his arrows come filled with muscle relaxants. When they pierce us, we slip into lethargy and spiritual brain fog, and we don't even know what hit us. Pause here and ask the Lord to show you if there are any areas of your spiritual walk where you've settled into a passive acceptance of your circumstances. A settling that's not born of faith but rather unbelief. Write out your thoughts.

Say NO! Sometimes when we settle in the land of unbelief, our hearts can become hardened there. The Israelites had a promise from God and past miracles to prove He meant what He said. Yet they eventually identified more with their discomforts and personal preferences than they did with the One True God, and their hard hearts became downright rebellious.

> The people refused to enter the pleasant land,
>   for they wouldn't believe his promise to care for them.
> Instead, they grumbled in their tents
>   and refused to obey the LORD.
>
> Psalm 106:24–25

Prayerfully ask God to show you times and places when you've said no to Him. If necessary, spend some time repenting and relinquishing your love of control. Then rise up and put your *no* where it belongs! ☺ Tell the enemy he will not steal your promised life from you! Write out a bold faith declaration below.

....

....

....

....

Say YES! For us to lift high our sword of the Spirit and say, "Oh, yes I will!" we need to know the things about which God has told us yes. Based on what you've read in Scripture (and even in this chapter), for what do you believe God has told you, *"Yes, My dear one. These are yours because you are Mine"*? What do you *know that you know* He has promised you? Even if your emotions haven't caught up with what Scripture says, and these things don't exactly feel true, it's okay. Let's start here. What exactly has God promised you? Write down what you know.

Personalized Prayer

Heavenly Father,

Thank You for loving and saving me! I KNOW I am loved! I know I am secure! Help me to believe You for greater measures of healing and wholeness. Lord, I believe. Help my unbelief. Awaken me to my specific God-given calling and give me the faith to lay hold of it. Open my eyes to the power of Your Word and show me specific promises that are mine for the taking. You've created me to live loved, and to walk by faith. Help me to know You more, that I might live the kingdom life You've made possible for me. I love You with my life. In Your name, I pray. Amen.

Spiritual Intelligence Training
PRESS ON, IN JESUS' NAME!

1. I've explored Ruth's story in previous books, but I must do so again. Her life inspires me so! Ruth was a Moabite widow. Moabites were enemies of the Jewish people because of their idolatry and their open willingness to sacrifice their children to the gods. But Ruth had married a Jewish man who lived in the land of Moab. Over time, Ruth came to know and love the God of Abraham. Eventually, Ruth's husband, brother-in-law, and father-in-law died, leaving her, her sister-in-law, and her mother-in-law, Naomi, destitute. All this loss had understandably propelled Naomi into a faith crisis, and it was Ruth's faith that saved them. Sometimes you need to borrow someone's faith when you don't have enough of your own. Read Ruth 1 and answer the following questions:

    a. Naomi spoke bitterly against God and blamed Him for her pain and loss (when in reality, it was her husband who led them outside of God's will to the land of Moab). We all speak out of our pain when life gets hard. Is there a time recently when you blamed God for the hardships in your life? Write it down.

    b. Ruth trusted in a God she could not see. And she was a woman of profound honor and character. Imagine the risk involved in this journey. Women (without men) were especially vulnerable in that day, and they risked their lives to make that trek. Ruth was leaving everything she knew. She was traveling with Naomi, the person who taught her about God. And who, at the moment, questioned all she knew about God. Put yourself in Ruth's shoes. What kinds of emotions might surface for you?

2. Faith mixed with action is the recipe for miracles. Read Ruth 2:1–9 and make a note of God's direction, protection, and provision. Boaz instructed Ruth to stay in his fields so she'd be safe. What protective boundaries has God established for you in this season of life?

3. Read Ruth 2:10–14 and notice how Ruth went from being a destitute widow to a worker in a field. Boaz promised to protect her, and he offered her more food than she could eat in one sitting. We can't know all of what God has prevented in our lives and how richly He has provided for us, but some things we do know. How has God moved you from one status to another, one circumstance to another? And in what ways has He provided more than you need?

4. Read Ruth 2:15–23 and notice again how Boaz orchestrated circumstances to provide for and protect Ruth. And *it just so happened* that Boaz was a close family relative (which would make him their kinsman redeemer). Time and time again, we see "templates" in Scripture for the ways God intervenes in our lives. Jesus stepped in as our Kinsman Redeemer. He also *so* delights in every detail of our lives that He arranges many "as it happened" moments for us. He leads us even when we're unaware.

   a. Ponder this passage from Psalm 37:23: "The LORD directs the steps of the godly. He delights in every detail of their lives." How have you found that to be true? Give an example.

   b. Pause here and write out a prayer thanking God for His divine intervention in your life. He's at work even when you can't see it or sense it.

5. Read Ruth 3 and ponder this question: How might God ask you to step up and step out to lay hold of the promise He's made? Do you trust Him? Write down your thoughts.

6. In Ruth chapter 4, we read how Boaz cunningly negotiated to marry Ruth. Imagine Ruth waiting expectantly to hear the news. Delays are always a part of the redemption story, yes? But did you notice how Naomi's faith came back to life because of Ruth's diligence and faithfulness to her and to God? Whose diligence and dedication inspire you today? And whose faith are you encouraging? Write down your thoughts.

7. Zero in on Ruth 4:13–15 and ponder how faithfully God redeemed this story for Naomi, Ruth, and Boaz! I'm about to ask you to do

something audacious. Write out your own version of what we read in verses 13–14; in other words, picture your friends surrounding you, celebrating with you, and praising God because He broke through for you. What might your breakthrough look like, and what would your friends have to say about it? Write down your thoughts.

TEN

It's Time to Trust Him More

Stay in Awe

———

Even if you have no more than just one promise from the Word of God, it is time to get up and go into the valley to face your giant saying, "You are not defying me, you are defying the God who created this universe. He has interwoven the very honor of His name in keeping and sustaining me, in using my life for His glory. You are defying the God who bought me with His blood 2,000 years ago!"[1]

Picture yourself behind enemy lines, running through the woods with great agility—ducking this way and then that. You're sprinting fast and efficiently, navigating the uneven terrain as you leap over logs and boulders. You find a clearing in the woods and see a raging river. But you never skip a beat or slow down. You keep running. Suddenly, an unseen hand propels you up and over the raging river to the other side. As soon as you land, you're propelled forward with new strength and power. Can you picture it? This is you in the spiritual realm.

Your trials have trained you. Your mountains have strengthened you. And your dependence upon God has deepened you. If you could see what God has accomplished in and through you as a result of your faith, you would release a holy roar and refuse to back down from another battle ever again. The enemy doesn't have endurance, but you do. The enemy doesn't have God on his side, but you do. The enemy isn't guaranteed a win, but you are. This faith journey isn't for sissies. (Well, actually, it is. But He makes warriors out of us eventually. ☺)

It's time to trust God for more. To believe Him for more. And to walk in the *more* that Jesus has for you.

One night I made the mistake of watching more news than I had the grace to process. I went to bed overwhelmed and defeated by the evil that prospers, the corruption that flourishes, and the seeming absence of justice in the land. How long before God would deal with the misuse of power? How long before He'd bring the truth to light? How long before He would show His enemies His zeal for His people?

> O God, listen to my cry!
>> Hear my prayer!
> From the ends of the earth,
>> I cry to you for help
>> when my heart is overwhelmed.
> Lead me to the towering rock of safety,
>> for you are my safe refuge,
>> a fortress where my enemies cannot reach me.
> Let me live forever in your sanctuary,
>> safe beneath the shelter of your wings!
>
> Psalm 61:1–4

I crawled into bed, curled up in a ball, and fell fast asleep. I had another one of those vivid dreams. In the dream, I stood up to my knees in vast chunks of rubble, a massive amount of debris spread over an area about the size of a football field.

The big chunks of concrete were from large, ornate buildings—halls of power. I stood there amidst this pile of concrete. The warmth of the sun shone down on me. I had a look of absolute and utter awe on my face. I couldn't believe what had just happened.

Your trials have **trained** you. Your mountains have **strengthened** you. And your dependence upon God has **deepened** you.

Off to my left, I could see a holy city—rows of actual halls of power that could not be destroyed. They had an orangish glow to them as though they were from another world.

In front of me, the warmth of the sun filled my soul. I looked over my shoulder and noticed that various men and women stood in the rubble about every twenty feet or so, with that same look of awe on their faces. We all looked at each other and then up to the sky with the same thought: *No way did that just happen!*

It was evident in the dream that we were all intercessors and these demolished structures represented all the misuses of power that had taken place on the earth. Our persistent prayers had brought down a massive infrastructure of corruption. We were puny humans, and these systems had seemed impenetrable, yet there we stood, in a pile of rubble that was far bigger than we were. We had overcome. God used the weak to shame the strong.

I woke up from this dream with a start. Energized, I sat up, and instantly joy and awe rose within me. I hurried out to my quiet place to read and pray and listen. Surges of faith and expectancy rose within me. God met me in that place. I was overwhelmed with a sense of His presence and the assurance that He sees all and one day will dismantle every evil scheme.

If that's what our prayers can do, we must pray more with greater fervency, specificity, and faith, wouldn't you say? God *moves* on the prayers of His people. He shakes, dismantles, untangles, confronts, and diffuses enemy schemes *because of our prayers*. That morning, after such a vivid dream, I looked down at my open Bible and read this incredible passage. Read it slowly and prayerfully.

> God is our refuge and strength,
>   always ready to help in times of trouble.
> So we will not fear when earthquakes come
>   and the mountains crumble into the sea.
> Let the oceans roar and foam.
>   Let the mountains tremble as the waters surge!

A river brings joy to the city of our God,
  the sacred home of the Most High.
God dwells in that city; it cannot be destroyed.
  From the very break of day, God will protect it.
The nations are in chaos,
  and their kingdoms crumble!
God's voice thunders,
  and the earth melts!
The LORD of Heaven's Armies is here among us;
  the God of Israel is our fortress.

Come, see the glorious works of the LORD:
  See how he brings destruction upon the world.
He causes wars to end throughout the earth.
  He breaks the bow and snaps the spear;
  he burns the shields with fire.

"Be still, and know that I am God!
  I will be honored by every nation.
  I will be honored throughout the world."

The LORD of Heaven's Armies is here among us;
  the God of Israel is our fortress.

Psalm 46

I know there are varying opinions as to whether God speaks through dreams, but I have to say, there's no doubt in my mind that God used this dream to infuse me with hope and expectancy. I went to bed discouraged and depressed, and I woke up filled with fiery faith. You couldn't steal my joy that day. I knew in my knower that God moves when we pray, and one day we will stand in absolute awe at His power and attention to detail.

The following day, I stumbled upon another passage.

O LORD, I will honor and praise your name,
  for you are my God.

You do such wonderful things!
    You planned them long ago,
    and now you have accomplished them.
You turn mighty cities into heaps of ruins.
    Cities with strong walls are turned to rubble.
Beautiful palaces in distant lands disappear
    and will never be rebuilt.
Therefore, strong nations will declare your glory;
    ruthless nations will fear you.

                    Isaiah 25:1–3

Pay attention to the awe expressed in the verses below:

In Jerusalem, the LORD of Heaven's Armies
    will spread a wonderful feast
    for all the people of the world.
It will be a delicious banquet
    with clear, well-aged wine and choice meat.
There he will remove the cloud of gloom,
    the shadow of death that hangs over the earth.
He will swallow up death forever!
    The Sovereign LORD will wipe away all tears.
He will remove forever all insults and mockery
    against his land and people.
    The LORD has spoken!

In that day the people will proclaim,
"This is our God!
    We trusted in him, and he saved us!
This is the Lord, in whom we trusted.
    Let us rejoice in the salvation he brings!"

                    Isaiah 25:6–9, emphasis mine

Picture yourself, standing in awe, with a dumbfounded look on your face, overwhelmed by the way God answered your accumulated prayers. Imagine standing with a throng of other believers, all shouting the words of Isaiah 25:9. "This is our God! We trusted in him, and he saved us! . . . Let us rejoice in the salvation He brings!"

Author and pastor Alan Wright joins me on the show occasionally. He said something one day that is still speaking to me: God's "Spirit, His breath, is in His words. . . . The Spirit of God and the Word of God are so intimately connected" that when God sends forth His Word, He sends forth Himself.[2] Wherever God's living Word goes, there He is. When we pray God's Word, we send forth His very breath and presence and power throughout the earth to accomplish His righteous and divine purposes on the earth. Makes me never want to waste another word again. I want to know His Word, speak His Word, pray His Word, and believe His Word.

How many times have we engaged with God, believed His Word, only to back off as soon as opposition arose? How many break-throughs have we narrowly missed because we lost heart in the battle? We actually need opposition in our lives, lest we grow soft, weak, and self-focused. Carter Conlon writes:

> Without opposition, the Church gets lazy—she turns inward and seeks power without purpose, which is a formula for spiritual de-lusion. When the Church comes to a place where she's no longer opposed, she declines. . . . You have a choice to make now. You can sit on the hillside and listen to the voice of your condemner for the rest of your life. . . . Or you can stand up and recognize the purpose of the opposition in your life. You can choose to believe that as you turn to God, He will give you the courage to face your enemies and triumph over them.[3]

What would happen if a holy roar arose within us and we decided we're not backing down? That instead we are determined to rise up, stand firm, and trust God to watch over His Word to perform it.[4]

Sometimes you just have to stomp your feet and tell that devil, "I am not moving from this place of faith! My God is with me, so you will not outlast me. I'm growing stronger in battle while you're getting weaker. If I determine not to quit, I will outlast you. Victory is mine, not yours!"

Picture yourself sitting at the table the Lord prepared for you on your battlefield. Imagine the table expands right before your eyes—to the left and the right, and out in front of you. The food suddenly multiplies exponentially. You realize that your battle—your victory—is about to nourish others.

Where there was one loaf of bread, you now have a basketful. Where there was a small plate of fruit, you've got a cornucopia bursting with many kinds of fruit. Where there was a chalice of wine, you now have enough for an army of believers. You envision your victory. It's within your reach!

Then you look up and notice that as your strength and provision grow, your enemy withers.

We can persevere. We must persevere. We will win in the end.

Patient endurance is what you need now, so that you will continue to do God's will. Then you will receive all that he has promised.

Hebrews 10:36

Mark Batterson writes:

I love the two-word phrase in Acts 10:3: *one day*. It is pregnant with hope. Why? Because one day could be today. Today could be the day that God answers the prayer, performs the miracle, or keeps the promise! In *one day*, God can deliver from an addiction that has held a person captive for years. In *one day*, God can bring a prodigal child who has run away and been gone for decades. In *one day*, God can provide more than someone has accumulated in a lifetime. But if we are going to experience a miracle *one day*, we need to pray every day. Too many people pray like they are playing the lottery. Prayer is more like an investment account. Every deposit accumulates compound interest. And *one day*, if we keep making deposits every day, it will pay in dividends beyond our wildest imagination.[5]

Here we are, on the home stretch of this journey. If you and I were out for lunch, I'd lean in, grab your arm, look you in the eye, and speak these words to you:

God has done a stunning work in you. He's used every trial, collected every tear, moved on every prayer, and multiplied every seed you've sown in faith. Though you've felt at times you were on your own, fighting for inches, you've gained miles in the spiritual realm. You're stronger than you feel because Christ is boldly and bravely alive in you!

You are a fierce warrior with a childlike spirit. There's still much inside you that God intends to heal, but you must trust Him in the process. He is working miracles in, through, and all around you. One day you'll see it. All of us right now see as in a glass dimly,[6] partly because we're still on the earth and partly because of our own pain filters and biased experiences. As you walk intimately with Jesus, He'll lift those pain filters one by one, and bring clarity to your spiritual vision.

There's a place in you that God wants to heal so deeply that it'll open your eyes to the wonder of your blessed life and to the magnificent gifts He's imparted to you. We often miss the best parts of our lives when we have unhealed areas in our souls. But God doesn't fault you for sometimes seeing unclearly. He is patient with you, so be patient with yourself. Your struggle through this life will only provide a stark contrast to the glory that will be revealed to you on that Great Day. Wait for it with joyful expectancy.

God sees all that's happening upon the earth today. He sees every heart and knows why people do the things they do. He's been as close as your very breath each time you bowed your head and prayed for the burdens of your heart. He loves the way you care for your family and for the world in which they live. He's never missed a moment with you. He's heard every single prayer and will one day soon pour out His Spirit so powerfully, so precisely, it will take your breath away.

211

Jesus saved you not to enslave you. He saved you because He loves you. He created you for a very distinct purpose, some of which you can discern right now, but parts of which have been hidden from you until the appropriate time. When it's time to step up, you'll be ready for it.

Stay focused on Jesus. Keep your heart engaged. Stand firmly on His Word. And trust Him with your loved ones. He cares deeply about them and is working in each of their lives. He is moving in nuanced ways that fit the timing of the greater story He's writing on the earth today. Their stories are more about His story than yours, although He knows how deeply personal this journey is for you.

Have no fear. Your journey—as painful as it has been at times— has served you well because it has forged these two critical components of kingdom warfare:

1. Deep compassion for those who suffer
2. A fierce warrior spirit

Many of God's children fight their battles in the flesh, which only strengthens the enemy's occupation in certain places. Yet the tenderizing work God has done in you because of the battles you've had to fight has moved God's purposes forward. God knows what He's doing with you! And no, you will not have to endure everything you fear. He will help you put an end to the continual state of threat within you. He will step in and do for you that which you cannot do for yourself. You will break through. You *are* breaking through.

Your journey has initiated faith and courage in more people than you can imagine. Your struggle has been real but has accomplished great things that you will one day see. God wants you to get to a place where you are more emboldened by the *fruit* of your suffering than you are paralyzed by your fears of the past.

The devil wants you to attach your present pain to past trauma so he can hold you captive. God wants you to attach your present pain to the future glory that awaits you so He can set you free.

God wants you
to get to a **place**
where you are
more emboldened
by the **fruit** of
your suffering than
you are paralyzed
by your **fears** of
the past.

Rise up, dear one! Trust God! There's more! So much more He wants to do in and through you. Keep your eyes fixed on Jesus. Remind your soul of His goodness and His faithfulness. Believe Him for great things. Be about His work. You do hear His voice, so respond to Him, even to the slightest nudge within you. He will faithfully guide you into all truth[7] and into places and spaces where He's working so you can join Him.

Keep your heart constantly before Him, pure and holy, faithful and true. Guard diligently against toxic, defeating, betraying, and fearful thoughts. Those things don't belong in the kingdom, and they don't belong in you. Rise up and believe Him, this very hour! He is about to do great things in our midst. Jesus loves you with so much love that you could never contain it in that little body of yours!

The infinite, star-breathing God lives inside of you! You carry this treasure in your earthen vessel, so you'll always know that the power that marks your life is from Him, not from you.[8] Believe it. Receive it. Walk in it.

Prayerful Reflective Questions

1. Lord, *where have I given up too soon? (Accept His grace and forgiveness here, but allow Him to speak to you about how to better stand in future battles.)*
2. *How has opposition impacted me for the better and for the worse? (You may have areas that God still wants to heal.)*
3. *How can I add my prayers with others' to see evil dismantled in the world today?*
4. *How have my battles trained me? What kind of warrior am I?*

The Humble Way: As the days grow more evil and the love of most grows cold, we must shine brighter and love deeper. We'll never have supernatural compassion for our enemies without being supernaturally connected to the Spirit of the living God. We'll never have the courage or the love to speak the truth unless that same Spirit of Truth is constantly operating in and refining us. We'll never possess otherworldly wisdom without knowing God's Word and walking in His ways. Yet that's what the world so desperately needs—His compassion, His love, His truth, and His wisdom.

For us to rightly reflect Christ in the coming days, we may need to die a thousand deaths. When others step on our toes, steal our thunder, or miss us completely, we need to remember who we are and love others where they are. Do you know what kind of maturity and insight that will require of us? Yet what we need is exactly who Jesus is, and how Jesus is, and praise God, He lives in us!

When we dare to step out in faith and we're met with open hostility, we must remember the saints who've gone before us and count ourselves in good company. When we go a long time before our prayers are answered, we must learn to have unwavering confidence in almighty God. We're fast becoming a remnant of Christ-followers, traveling to a Holy City, while the rest of the world rushes in the opposite direction.

From now until Jesus returns, we must decrease that He might increase in us. And that's not something to fear, but rather, it is something to wholeheartedly embrace. Jesus is alive in us! As His influence grows exponentially within us, His power operates supernaturally through us.

Spend some time here and talk with God about this process of decrease and increase. Humble yourself before Him. Trust Him to take care of you. Then ask Him to display such power through you

215

that you begin to see waters parted, mountains moved, and lives restored. Write out your prayerful thoughts here.

Discern the Fiery Arrows: One of the poisonous arrows the enemy repeatedly sends our way comes with a question: *Is God trustworthy?* He's absolutely worthy of our trust. We know this in our heads. But our hearts don't always discern or embrace this truth. Or maybe we discern the truth easily enough, but *persevering* in it when the battle rages on? Well, that's another thing altogether.

One of the ways you know that this arrow has hit its mark is if you live always bracing for impact. If, when you look to the heavens, you see a boot (the other shoe about to drop) instead of a hand reaching out to you, you might have an arrow tip that needs to be extracted from your soul.

Sometimes we think that if we could just go through several seasons in a row without crisis or hardship, we'd trust God more. And there's something to be said about that. Moses cried out, "Make us glad for as many days as you have afflicted us!"[9] Counselors also admit that one of the ways our hearts actually heal is when we're able to experience redemptive moments and make new memories in the very areas of our lives where we've been hurt or traumatized. And the thing is, it's God who brings about these scenarios *so we can heal*. But the question as to whether or not God is good isn't

216

settled by our ever-changing experiences. It's decided in our hearts through faith.

Spend some time here and ask the Lord to show you if there are still wounds in your soul for which you're holding God accountable. Ask Him to tend to those. Then engage your heart with His and determine to stand in faith. Tell Him and your own soul, *My God is good, and I trust Him with my whole heart.* Write out this passage of Scripture in your own words, specific to your story.

> Trust in the LORD with all your heart;
> > do not depend on your own understanding.
> Seek his will in all you do,
> > and he will show you which path to take.
>
> Don't be impressed with your own wisdom.
> > Instead, fear the LORD and turn away from evil.
> Then you will have healing for your body
> > and strength for your bones.
>
> Proverbs 3:5–8

Say NO! One of the things I learned about myself while writing this book is that even though I know how to use my *NO* in warfare, I've still put up with too much from the enemy of my soul. I've realized countless ways he has trespassed on my territory because I've allowed it. Something awakened in me, and I've been relentless with fighting back against the lies and the threats that have pummeled me for so long. I feel as though I've been engaged in hand-to-hand combat throughout this season, but guess what? I'm getting more robust, and the enemy is losing his power in my life.

There are some things God has promised me that I'm going after, and I won't relent until I've laid hold of them. But first, I needed to identify the places in my life where, instead of experiencing abundance, I endured the enemy's constant and continual thievery.

So how about you? Do you live without peace or joy? Because those belong to us in Christ Jesus. Do you feel constantly self-aware, and not in a good way? For instance, do you find yourself scanning your emotions with each new circumstance? Do your repeated thoughts keep you looking inward instead of upward? Does your self-talk reveal either an obsession with your feelings or with your deficits and weaknesses? Because that's a sign the enemy has been given real estate that's not his to claim. Is fear constantly knocking at your door? Because you have an answer for that uninvited guest.

My battle, as you probably know, has been mainly centered around my health. When scary symptoms surged and I'd count the years I've endured this struggle (thirty, to be precise), I'd lose heart and continually beg God for mercy and a miracle. I'd sometimes feel hurt that He has allowed this to go on as long as it has. I'd default to places of fear, terror, and discouragement. It's no wonder I lost so many skirmishes with the enemy. Sometimes I'd battle well and win, but it always felt like two steps forward and three steps back.

When I stopped begging and started believing, something shifted within me. When I identified despair, terror, and even discouragement as from the pit of hell, meant to derail me, I rose up and sent those things back where they belong. Years ago, I decided to practice a zero-tolerance policy on fear. Since then, I've used that policy with every thought process that contradicted God's Word. Why? Because any thought process that runs contrary to God's promises weakens us. I've had to be relentless. But I'm gaining ground.

All of that to say, *Is it time for you to trust Him more?* Pause here and ask God to show you places where the enemy has presumed upon your hospitality. It's time for him to leave. Picture your enemy being shoved off of your land—no more occupation. Imagine having an abundance of peace instead. Prayerfully meditate on the following verse and then write down your thoughts:

> For yet a little while and the wicked one will be gone [forever];
> Though you look carefully where he used to be, he will not
> be [found].
>
> But the humble will [at last] inherit the land
> And will delight themselves in abundant prosperity and
> peace.
>
> Psalm 37:10–11 AMP

Say YES! You are loved, called, and empowered. Culture is shifting all around us, but some things will not be moved! God's love. God's promises. And God's commitment to carry out His purposes on the earth and in your life.

Are you ready to give God your *YES* without knowing fully what He's asking of you? We can only do that when we trust that God is a good Father and that He withholds no good thing from those who walk uprightly before Him. Spend some time pondering God's goodness, and then, when you're ready, give Him your yes and get moving. Take the next steps as He directs and expect to see Him not only move in your midst but also to surprise you with His goodness. From now on, you'll see opposition as an opportunity to witness God's power. And you'll be changed from the inside out.

> Whether the barrier is a river, a mountain, or a gate, all a child of Jesus must do is head directly toward it. If it is a river, it will dry up as he comes near it, as long as he still forges ahead. If it is a mountain, it will be removed and "cast into the sea" (Mark 11:23), providing he approaches it with unflinching confidence.[10]

Spend some time here aligning your heart with your heavenly Father's. When you're ready, give Him your yes. Write out your prayer here.

Personalized Prayer

Lord God Almighty,

You are everything to me! I stretch out my hands, look up to the heavens, and ask You to do the impossible in and through me! Father, help me to live a life worthy of Your name. Forgive me for allowing the enemy space in my life that he doesn't deserve. Put a new fire within me to stand in faith, raise my shield, and claim my assigned territory. As the world grows dark, shine brightly through me. I want to pray for the sick and see them recover. I want to speak with such authority that the rejected know they're accepted, the lost are finally found, and the righteous are mobilized to carry out their high calling in You. Awaken fresh faith in me. No more hiding, no more passivity, no more unrighteous self-protection. I'm done with those. In You and by Your Spirit, I am anointed and appointed. I am bold and brave. And I will stand with You on that final day. Thank You for loving me, for saving me, and for awakening me with Your Spirit. I cannot wait to see You face-to-face. Help me to last long and finish strong. In Your matchless name, I pray. Amen.

Spiritual Intelligence Training
JESUS OVERCAME, WE WILL OVERCOME

1. It was almost time for Jesus to go to the cross, and He prepared His disciples for the journey ahead. He prayed for them. And He prayed for us. Read John 17, noting the themes in this chapter, and write down your thoughts (e.g., God's glory, unity, and holiness). What stands out to you here?

2. Jesus, the Son of God and King of the universe, was about to be arrested. Read John 18:1–10 and answer the following questions:

   a. When Jesus said, "I am He," the power of God burst forth and knocked the soldiers to the ground. Why is this such an important scene in the story?

   b. Peter—the passionate warrior—stepped in and defended Jesus. He sliced off the ear of the high priest's slave. But Jesus told him to put away his sword. My friend Jodi Ruch once said, "We know we have authority over our enemy. But sometimes we think we have authority over God." In other words, we fight against His ultimate plan. Is there a place in your life where you're fighting *against* God's ultimate purposes? Write down your thoughts.

3. Read John 19 and zero in on verse 11; in the worst parts of His trial, Jesus held fast to who He was and the power He possessed as the Son of God.

   a. Which of your trials has made you most doubt who you are in Christ Jesus?

   b. What has most helped you to understand who you are in Christ Jesus?

4. Jesus died on the cross, but then He rose from the grave! Read John 20:1–29 and consider this note from my NLT Study Bible: "The stone was not rolled aside so Jesus could get out, but so others could get in and see that Jesus had indeed risen from the dead, just as He had

promised."[11] No obstacle could ever hinder Jesus from getting to us and from carrying out His ultimate purposes for our lives. He rose from the grave! You are infinitely *blessed* when you believe before you see. One day, when you see Jesus face-to-face, you'll understand in the depths of your being all you've been forgiven, all that's been redeemed, and all that He saved you for. You've been grafted into a royal family.

    a. What obstacles do you need to move out of the way?

    b. What do you believe God for right now?

5. Let's read John 20:30–31 (emphasis mine) together: "The disciples saw Jesus do many other miraculous signs in addition to the *ones recorded in this book. But these are written so that you may continue to believe that Jesus is the Messiah, the Son of God, and that by believing in him you will have life by the power of his name.*" The Greek word for *life* in this passage is *zóé*, which means possessing vitality; the absolute fullness of life; "life active and vigorous, devoted to God, blessed, in the portion even in this world of those who put their trust in Christ, but after the resurrection, to be consummated by new accessions (among them, a more perfect body), and to last forever."[12] Write out a prayer declaring your trust in the Messiah, asking Him by faith to help you lay hold of the *life* He purchased for you!

6. God often provides us with full-circle moments. He brings us back to places of hurt, hardship, or failure so He can renew us and restore us. Jesus did this very thing for Peter. Read John 21 and picture Peter hastily jumping out of the boat to get to Jesus. Imagine him sitting by the charcoal fire with Jesus (a fresh reminder of where he was when he denied Christ). Jesus made a point to single out Peter and affirm their relationship.

    a. What do you suppose Peter felt at that moment?

    b. Have you experienced a full-circle moment in your life? What did you learn about God from that experience?

7. Jesus promised us that we would see trouble on the earth, but He told us to cheer up because He has overcome the world.[13] Here's our

last order of business together: Stand up, stretch out your arms, and declare out loud:

As a citizen of the heavenly kingdom,
An heir of God and joint-heir with Christ,
Filled with the Spirit of the Living God,
I speak with precision,
I pray with power,
I walk in authority.
I am anointed and appointed,
Blessed and beloved,
Bold and brave,
Called and courageous,
Because I know God is with me.
I will triumph over my enemy,
And I will stand with Jesus on that final day.

A FINAL NOTE
TO THE READER

Dear friend,

Thank you for making this journey with me! I pray God used it to equip and encourage you. Know that I'll be praying for you in the coming days. I can't wait to sit down with you at the Marriage Supper of the Lamb and hear about all of your heroic exploits. Many victories await you, my friend! And soon, we'll be home. Stay courageous. Until that day . . .

In Christ Jesus,

Susie Larson

Appendix

CORES OF CHRISTIANITY

We believe in one eternal God, Creator and Lord of the world, Father, Son, and Holy Spirit, who governs all things according to the purpose of His will. We affirm the divine inspiration, truthfulness, and authority of both Old and New Testament Scriptures in their entirety as the only written Word of God, without error in all that it affirms, and the only infallible rule of faith and practice.

We affirm that there is only one Savior and only one gospel, although there is a wide diversity of evangelistic approaches. To evangelize is to spread the good news that Jesus Christ died for our sins and was raised from the dead according to the Scriptures, and that, as the reigning Lord, He now offers the forgiveness of sins and the liberating gifts of the Spirit to all who repent and believe.

We affirm that God is both the Creator and the Judge of all men. We therefore should share His concern for justice and reconciliation throughout human society and for the liberation of men and women from every kind of oppression. Because men and women are made in the image of God, every person, regardless of race, religion, color, culture, class, sex, or age, has an intrinsic dignity, because of which he or she should be respected and served, not exploited.

We affirm that Christ sends His redeemed people into the world as the Father sent Him, and that this calls for a similar deep and costly penetration of the world. We affirm that the church's visible unity in truth is God's purpose.

We believe that we are engaged in constant spiritual warfare with the principalities and powers of evil, who are seeking to overthrow the church and frustrate its task of world evangelization. We know our need to equip ourselves with God's armor and to fight this battle with the spiritual weapons of truth and prayer.

We believe in the power of the Holy Spirit. The Father sent His Spirit to bear witness to His Son; without His witness, ours is futile. Conviction of sin, faith in Christ, new birth, and Christian growth are all His work.

We believe that Jesus Christ will return personally and visibly, in power and glory, to consummate His salvation and His judgment. This promise of His coming is a further spur to our evangelism, for we remember His words that the gospel must first be preached to all nations.

ACKNOWLEDGMENTS

To Andy McGuire: You are so much more than an editor; you're a brilliant mind, a deep heart, and a dear friend. I can't imagine making this journey without you. Thank you for helping me steward the words God has given me to share. Sharon Hodge, thank you for sharing your editorial expertise and for bringing such excellence to this project!

To Mark Rice, Deirdre Close, Rod Jantzen, and the BHP Marketing Team: Thank you, thank you for your heart for the things of God and for the work you put into getting our books out into the world. Yours is not an easy job. I appreciate you!

To Steve Laube: Thank you for always being only a phone call away. ☺

To my sample readers: Lynn, Bonnie, Janet, Daryl, Judy, Brooke, Krista, Sarah, Ted and Les, Kathy, Renee, and Karen: Thank you for taking the time to work through my content with me. Your feedback encouraged me greatly!

To my kids—Jake and Lizzie, Luke and Kristen, Jordan and Jiethyl—and grandbabies: You are my priceless treasures, straight from God's heart to mine. May you continue to grow in the knowledge of His love and stand firm in the promises He has made. Love you forever.

To my dear husband, Kev: There's no way I'd be the person I am today if not for the way God has used you in my life. You represent His heart so well. You make His heart visible, His love tangible, and His promises believable. Thank you so much. Love you, honey.

To My Jesus: Jesus, You're the first one I think about in the morning and the last one I talk to at night. You've been so faithful, Lord. How can I ever thank You enough for loving me, saving me, and changing me from the inside out? I count the days until I can see You face-to-face. Until then, grant me the courage and conviction to finish well. Thank You, Lord.

NOTES

Introduction

1. Thann Bennett, *My Fame, His Fame : Aiming Your Life and Influence Toward the Glory of God* (Nashville, TN: Thomas Nelson, 2020), 63–64.

Chapter 1: The Battle Is Real

1. *Life Application Study Bible: New Living Translation* (Carol Stream, IL: Tyndale House, 2007), Ephesians 2:2 study note, 2615.

2. Paraphrase of lyrics from "Never Lost a Battle," written by Steven Furtick, Chris Brown, and Tiffany Hammer; Elevation Worship Records, 2019.

3. See Romans 8:28.

4. See James 4:7.

5. If you don't have any study helps handy, you can do a Google search and find plenty of verses on your specific topic.

6. *New Spirit-Filled Life Bible, NKJV* (Nashville, TN: Thomas Nelson, 2002), 192.

Chapter 2: Why Am I Facing Attack?

1. Ray Pritchard, *Stealth Attack: Protecting Yourself Against Satan's Plan to Destroy Your Life* (Chicago, IL: Moody Publishers, 2007), 57.

2. Bo Stern, *Beautiful Battlefields* (Colorado Springs, CO: NavPress, 2013), 34.

3. Charles Wesley, "And Can It Be That I Should Gain," hymn, 1738.

4. My paraphrase of Psalm 139:23–24.

5. See Isaiah 55:8–9.

Chapter 3: Whose Side Are You On?

1. Francis Frangipane, *Holiness, Truth, and the Presence of God* (Cedar Rapids, IA: Arrow Publications, 1986), 54.

2. This content on Joshua was previously published in my book *Prevail: 365 Days of Enduring Strength from God's Word* (Bloomington, MN: Bethany House, 2020), 51.

3. This visual is not my original thought. I've heard it used by various communicators over the years and am not sure of the original source.

4. See Joel 2:13.

5. *Life Application Study Bible: New Living Translation* (Carol Stream, IL: Tyndale House, 1996, 2004, 2007), 562–563, emphases mine.

Chapter 4: Wisdom in the Off-Season

1. Bo Stern, *Ruthless: Knowing the God Who Fights for You* (Colorado Springs, CO: NavPress, 2014), 123–124.

2. I do realize I've already included this verse in the book, but you may see it a few more times. This is a powerful truth we need imprinted on our souls!

3. Tessa Afshar, *Jewel of the Nile* (Carol Stream, IL: Tyndale, 2021), 257–258.

4. If you need some inner healing, check out my book *Fully Alive: Learning to Flourish—Mind, Body & Spirit* (Bethany House, 2018).

5. This insight was shared by author and pastor Jeff Manion, who has been a guest on my show several times.

6. Dr. Warren Wiersbe, *The Wiersbe Bible Commentary, New Testament* (Colorado Springs, CO: David C. Cook, 2007), 622.

7. Roy Hession, *When I Saw Him: Where Revival Begins* (Fort Washington, PA: CLC Publications, 1975), 50–51.

8. See Song of Solomon 2:15.

9. Paul Hurckman on *Susie Larson Live*, March 31, 2021.

Chapter 5: What's Discernment?

1. Dr. David Ireland, *The Weapon of Prayer: Maximize Your Greatest Strategy Against the Enemy* (Lake Mary, FL: Charisma House, 2015), 177.

2. Oswald Chambers, *My Utmost for His Highest* (New York: Dodd, Mead & Company, 1956), 165.

3. *Life Application Study Bible: New Living Translation* (Carol Stream, IL: Tyndale House, 1996, 2004, 2007), Romans 14:10 study note, 2508.

4. See Matthew 7:15.

5. See Revelation 2:4–5.

6. See 1 Corinthians 13:7; James 1:19; 2 Corinthians 5:16; James 2:13.

7. See 1 Corinthians 13:12.

8. See Ephesians 4:3.

9. Though often attributed to St. Augustine of Hippo, the phrase is not found in his extant writings and is more recently credited to seventeenth-century German theologian Rupertus Meldenius, with another possible source being Marco Antonio De Dominis. See https://faculty.georgetown.edu/jod/augustine/quote.html and https://www.ligonier.org/learn/articles/essentials-unity-non-essentials-liberty-all-things.

10. Interlinear Bible Search, StudyLight.org., 1 Corinthians 12:10.

11. Philippians 1:9.

12. See 1 Corinthians 11:28.

13. See Romans 12:2.

14. *Streams in the Desert*, comp. L.B. Cowman (Grand Rapids, MI: Zondervan, 1997), 158.

15. Dr. Warren Wiersbe, *The Wiersbe Bible Commentary, New Testament* (Colorado Springs, CO: David C. Cook, 2007), 374.

Chapter 6: Navigating the Long Battle

1. Mark Batterson, *Whisper: How to Hear the Voice of God* (Carol Stream, IL: Tyndale House, 2017), 114.

2. See Psalm 73:26.

3. John Eldredge on *Susie Larson Live*, February 1, 2021.

4. See 2 Corinthians 13:5; Colossians 1:27; Galatians 2:20; Romans 8:11; Ephesians 2:5.

5. Dr. Jack Hayford, *NKJV New Spirit-Filled Life Bible* (Nashville, TN: Thomas Nelson, 2002), 362, italics mine.

6. See Romans 8:26.

Chapter 7: You Have an Enemy

1. Samuel Rodriguez, *Persevere with Power: What Heaven Starts, Hell Cannot Stop* (Minneapolis, MN: Chosen Books, 2021), 28.

2. See Psalm 24:9.

3. See John 4:34.

4. There is so much power packed into this and the preceding scriptural promises. See Isaiah 53:5; Romans 5:9; Revelation 12:11; and 1 John 4:18.

5. See Matthew 13:23 and Mark 4:20.

6. Francis Frangipane, *Holiness, Truth, and the Presence of God* (Cedar Rapids, IA: Arrow Publications, 1986), 59.

Chapter 8: Guard Your Heart

1. Louie Giglio, *Don't Give the Enemy a Seat at Your Table* (Nashville, TN: W Publishing, 2021), 152.

2. See Genesis 25.

3. *New Spirit-Filled Life Bible New Living Translation* (Nashville, TN: Thomas Nelson, 2002, 2013), "Word Wealth on Ephesians 6:13," 1543.

4. See 2 Samuel 11.

5. Kyle Strobel on *Susie Larson Live*, April 19, 2021.

Chapter 9: Contend for the Promises

1. Kevin Butcher, *Free: Rescued from Shame-Based Religion, Released into the Life-Giving Love of Jesus* (Colorado Springs, CO: NavPress, 2021), 103.

2. My paraphrase. Read the story in 1 Kings 18.

3. See Luke 10:20.

4. See Colossians 1:13.

5. See Ephesians 3:19.

6. See John 10:28.

7. Dr. Tim Jennings suggested this exercise several times on my show (including on March 25, 2021).

8. Dane Ortlund, *Gentle and Lowly: The Heart of Christ for Sinners and Sufferers* (Wheaton, IL: Crossway, 2020), 31.

9. Jurgen Moltmann, *The Way of Jesus Christ: Christology in Messianic Dimensions*, trans. M. Kohl (Minneapolis, MN: Fortress, 1993), 98, as quoted in Ortlund, *Gentle and Lowly*. Similarly, Graeme Goldsworthy, *The Son of God and the New Creation*, Short Studies in Biblical Theology (Wheaton, IL: Crossway, 2015), 43.

Chapter 10: It's Time to Trust Him More

1. Carter Conlon, *Fear Not: Living Courageously in Uncertain Times* (Bloomington, MN: Bethany House, 2012), 141.

2. Pastor Alan Wright on *Susie Larson Live*, May 21, 2021.

3. Conlon, *Fear Not*, 140–141.

4. See Jeremiah 1:12.

5. Mark Batterson, *Draw the Circle: The 40 Day Prayer Challenge* (Grand Rapids, MI: Zondervan, 2012), 78.

6. See 1 Corinthians 13:12.

7. See John 16:13.

8. See 2 Corinthians 4:7–9.

9. Psalm 90:15 ESV.

10. *Streams in the Desert*, comp. L. B. Cowman (Grand Rapids, MI: Zondervan, 1997), 258.

11. *Life Application Study Bible: New Living Translation* (Carol Stream, IL: Tyndale House, 1996, 2004, 2007), Matthew 28:2 study note, 2089.

12. "2222. zóé," *Thayer's Greek Lexicon* at Bible Hub, https://biblehub.com/thayers/2222.htm.

13. John 16:33.

Susie Larson is a national speaker, a bestselling author, and the host of the daily talk show *Susie Larson Live*, heard on the Faith Radio Network. Susie has written eighteen books and many articles. She's been a guest on *Focus on the Family*, the *Life Today* show, *Family Life Today*, as well as many other media outlets. Twice voted a top-ten finalist for the John C. Maxwell Transformational Leadership Award, she is also a veteran of the fitness field. Susie has been married to her dear husband, Kevin, since 1985, and together they have three wonderful sons, three beautiful daughters-in-law, three beautiful grandchildren, and one adorable pit bull named Memphis. Susie's passion is to see people everywhere awakened to the value of their soul, the depth of God's love, and the height of their calling in Christ Jesus.

More from Susie Larson

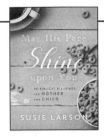

In this beautifully designed collection of 90 blessings—for both mother and child—Susie Larson provides hope-filled biblical declarations so both of you can receive strength and nourishment for your souls. Speak life into your children, sowing God's Word into their hearts as you also are rooted in the promises of God.

May His Face Shine upon You

In the hurriedness of December, it's easy to forget about the sacredness of the season. What if you approached this Advent season with an open heart and room for God? *Prepare Him Room* invites you to give God sacred space in your holiday season, and gives you time to ponder the miracle of Christ within you and respond to His astonishing work in your life.

Prepare Him Room

Everything God asks of us is for our good and His glory. But that doesn't mean life is easy, and sometimes we need to be reminded of God's power over all we face. In this inspiring devotional, Susie Larson offers 365 days' worth of opportunities for you to strengthen your walk in faith while finding a new level of freedom and redemption.

Prevail

⬧BETHANYHOUSE

Stay up to date on your favorite books and authors with our free e-newsletters. Sign up today at bethanyhouse.com.

 facebook.com/BHPnonfiction

 @bethany_house

 @bethany_house_nonfiction